Quarter Notes

Charles Wright

Quarter Notes

IMPROVISATIONS AND INTERVIEWS

Ann Arbor

THE UNIVERSITY OF MICHIGAN PRESS

for Justin d'Aldoce, who knows Bliss by another name . . .
—Appreciation of days gone by—

Copyright © by the University of Michigan 1995
All rights reserved
Published in the United States of America by
The University of Michigan Press
Manufactured in the United States of America
♾ Printed on acid-free paper

2001   2000   1999   1998   5   4   3   2

A CIP catalog record for this book is available from the British Library.

Library of Congress Cataloging-in-Publication Data
Wright, Charles, 1935–
    Quarter notes : improvisations and interviews / Charles Wright.
        p.   cm.
    Includes bibliographical references and index.
    ISBN 0-472-09604-4 (hardcover : alk. paper).—ISBN 0-472-06604-8
(paperback : alk. paper)
    1. Wright, Charles, 1935–   —Interviews.   2. Poets,
American—20th century—Interviews.   3. Poetry—History and
criticism.   4. Poetry—Authorship.   5. Poetics.   I. Title.
PS3573.R52Z468   1995
811'.54—dc20   95-19281
                                                                          CIP

Acknowledgments

Grateful acknowledgment is made to the following journals and publishers for permission to reprint previously published material:

Field for "With Father Hopkins on Lake Como," *Field,* #43 (Fall 1990).

The Gettysburg Review for "Miseducation of the Poet," *The Gettysburg Review,* 6, no. 1 (Winter, 1993); for "Narrative of the Image."

The Iron Mountain Review for "Bytes and Pieces," *The Iron Mountain Review,* 8 (Spring 1992); for "Language, Landscape, and the Idea of God: A Conversation," 8 (Spring 1992).

The North Carolina Literary Review for "ET & WNC Express Lines," *The North Carolina Literary Review,* 2, no. 1 (Spring 1994).

The Ohio Review for "Titleism," *The Ohio Review,* #48 (1992); for "The Hydrosyllabic Foot."

The Paris Review for "The Art of Poetry XLI, Charles Wright," *The Paris Review* 113 (Winter II, 1989).

The Southern Review for "The Poem as Journey," *The Southern Review,* 29, no. 2 (Spring 1993); for "Homage to the Thin Man."

Verse for "Jump Hog or Die," *Verse,* 8, no. 3/9, no. 1 (Winter/Spring, 1992).

Preface

I tend to think of *Quarter Notes* as an extension, a long coda, if you will, to my previous collection of prose pieces, *Halflife,* a kind of *Halflife II.* I had called the first book *Halflife* on the presumption that prose had a faster half-life than poetry, as well as having only half the life that poetry does. Be that as it may, it still remains my weaker suit, I'm afraid, no matter how much intensity I give to its writing, or tenderness to its care and feeding. The fact is, of course, that I write this prose as I write my poems—in bursts and often discontinuous narrative, in short and often nonsequential stories. I find this an odd practice, and thus, as such things go, have tried to make a strength out of a weakness. The interview form, especially when written instead of spoken, I find particularly congenial to my thought pattern, which is why I continue to include interviews in a format perhaps better suited to more traditional prose. Also, what I call Improvisations, nonlinear, associational story lines, fit my manner better than flow-through essays might, were I capable of them.

So, the types of things one found in *Halflife* one will find in *Quarter Notes,* brief things, shorter things, but things that gather, I hope, to a kind of fullness, things that this time around are better minded and better appointed. The one exception to the *Halflife II* palimpsest is the correspondence with Charles Simic in part 2, conducted through the winter and spring of 1994. Such an exchange seemed to fit both our manners, it turned out, and we had a lot of fun with it. In fact, I've had fun with all of this, or I wouldn't have done it in the first place.

Contents

1

Miseducation of the Poet

Prologue

First, two assumptions: one, a life is not a story; two, the poet's "life" consists of only those things that are not good enough to go into his poems. Thus, part of a life is not part of a story, and the parts that I have been able to pick up and brush off here either are not poem-worthy or were overlooked by the searchlight I have stabbed from time to time into earlier areas of my life.

Second, I want to quote a couple of paragraphs from *Their Heads Are Green and Their Hands Are Blue,* by Paul Bowles. Substitute the phrase "the past" for "the Sahara" both times it appears and you will understand the landscape and geography I am about to talk about.

> Immediately when you arrive in the Sahara, for the first or the tenth time, you notice the stillness. An incredible, absolute silence prevails outside the towns; and within, even in busy places like the markets, there is a hushed quality in the air, as if the quiet were a conscious force which, resenting the intrusion of sound, minimizes and disperses sound straightaway. Then there is the sky, compared to which all other skies seem faint-hearted efforts. Solid and luminous, it is always the focal point of the landscape. At sunset, the precise, curved shadow of the earth rises into it swiftly from the horizon, cutting it into light section and dark section. When all daylight is gone, and the space is thick with stars, it is still of an intense and burning blue, darkest directly overhead and paling toward the earth, so that the night never really grows dark.

> You leave the gate of the fort or the town behind, pass the

camels lying outside, go up into the dunes, or out onto the hard, stony plain and stand awhile, alone. Presently, you will either shiver and hurry back inside the walls, or you will go on standing there and let something very peculiar happen to you, something that everyone who lives there has undergone and which the French call *le baptême de la solitude*. It is a unique sensation, and it has nothing to do with loneliness. . . . Here, in this wholly mineral landscape lighted by stars like flares, . . . nothing is left but your own breathing and the sound of your heart beating. A strange, and by no means pleasant, process of reintegration begins inside you, and you have the choice of fighting against it, and insisting on remaining the person you have always been, or letting it take its course. For no one who has stayed in the Sahara for a while is quite the same as when he came.

I. *Christ School*

Dirty Dancing is the story of a young girl's loss of innocence, a "rite of passage" film revolving around a few weeks in the summer of 1963 in a Catskills' resort. The girl, played by Jennifer Grey, has just graduated from high school and is going to enter Mount Holyoke College at the end of the summer. Of course she falls in love with the resort's chief dance instructor. Everyone lets everyone else down in small ways, but in the end—as we expect from such a movie—all is righted. In a peripheral but important way, the movie is also about dancing. Just before the closing dance number, Jack Weston, who plays the owner of the resort, turns to his long-time band leader and says: "It's all over. This sort of thing isn't going to happen anymore. . . ." But what, in the summer of 1963, was "all over"? What was not going to happen this way anymore?

That is what I want to tell you about. Precisely what was not going to happen anymore is what I, ten years earlier, in May, 1953, walked into as I left the Christ School chapel, in Arden, North Carolina. With graduation over and the sun streaming, in my gray suit and Full Cleveland (white tie, white belt, white shoes), I walked down the chapel stairs into No Sweat, an enormous country that existed in the ten-year time warp between the end of the Korean War and the death of John F. Kennedy. Jennifer Grey talked of the Peace Corps; we talked about Myrtle Beach. She lived and danced out the fantasies we had to be content merely to harbor. No Sweat was a country where things took care of themselves by natural selection and by natural progression. My progression, as I recall, was one of gravity, the route of choice for many of my generation—soon to be dubbed "The Silent Generation." Gravity meant for me a summer working on the hometown newspaper in Kingsport, Tennessee, four years at Davidson College (a period I have described elsewhere as "a time of amnesia"), another four years in the Army, and then two years of graduate school. At the very moment Jack Weston followed up his first two sentences with a third—"Families are not going to come to places like this anymore—all the kids want to go to Europe"—I was, in fact, beginning a two-year stint as a Fulbright student in Italy. Jack Weston was right in all three of his sentences—the period from 1953 to 1963 was another country indeed.

Before going on, I need to rewind my film a couple of years, back to the fall of 1951. But who can remember how it was to be sixteen when you are fifty-five? Incidents, yes; details, sometimes; people, occasionally (or, at least, the people you thought they were). But *the way it was, what it was like,* is something we make up, something we reconstruct and reinvent to suit our purposes. Which is all right, I think; certainly it is easier on the ego, an organ that takes quite a pummeling at the ages around sixteen and seventeen.

In 1951 Christ School was a kind of deliverance for me. The previous year, my fifteenth, I had spent at a place called Sky Valley School, with a student body of eight souls, seven boys and one girl. Two thousand acres up around Mount Pinnacle, outside Hendersonville, North Carolina. Eight kids under the evangelical thumb of the daughter of the Episcopal Bishop of South Carolina. Age fifteen is on the outer perimeter of appreciation for such surroundings, so when I saw a school with more than one building, not to mention 143 other students, I felt I had been released.

It has been said that every one of us preserves from his

past, from memories, from quotations by which he lives, no more than a few words salvaged from a receding lifetime. If this is true, three of the words I will remember are *Campus, Claim,* and *Crumb,* the notorious three C's that augmented the three R's in my days at Christ School. They comprised the ultimate punishment short of expulsion operative in those days: restriction to *Campus,* work on a *Claim* until it was finished, and waiting on tables (removing the *Crumbs*) for the duration of the punishment.

Incidents, details, people. Surely the biggest incident— and, I now think, a fortuitous one—was the discovery of a roll of Life Savers in my dresser drawer by a nosy prefect after my first Monday afternoon in town. (We had Mondays off and went to classes on Saturdays—no doubt to avoid as much "town confrontation" as possible on Saturday afternoons.) I was, of course, immediately given an oak tree to remove (the *Claim*), a table to wait on, and an unrelieved restriction to the campus until said tree was on the ground. I learned about the school in a hurry and, as it turned out, the school learned about me in a hurry. It was the old "throw 'em in and see if they can swim" theory. By the time the tree came down, with volunteers from Fourth, Fifth, and Sixth Cottages (living facilities for Upper Formers, eight boys to a cottage) hanging on ropes tied high in the tree and pushing on the trunk, I had become a member of the school in a way that little else would have made possible short of having a passing arm like John Elway's. The ordeal of agony is thicker than water. My one additional transgression during this several-week-long ordination was the liberation of Mr. Dave's axe one morning after breakfast as I was heading for my *Claim* to get in a few licks before classes. It was leaning against the doorjamb of the dining hall. Mr. Dave (about whom more later) was David Page Harris, Headmaster, teacher, and Supreme Deity of Christ School for many years: a truly remarkable man whose dedication and practices influenced the hundreds of boys who passed beneath his hands. In any case, when my roommate (who had been at the school much longer than I) asked where I had found such a fine cutting implement, and I told him, he visibly paled as he said: "That's The Man's axe." I needed no further encouragement and had it back in place before Himself had finished his breakfast coffee.

Is it not wonderful how full of self-love memory is? Two more floes break loose from the frozen part of that first year, one another incident, the other a detail.

One of the really great things about a place like Christ School was that you could play ball even if you were not very good, which was my case: I could not see very well, but I was slow, as the saying goes. I was first-team varsity on the baseball and basketball teams both years I was there. In baseball my first year, I got one hit during the entire season. In my senior year as a starting guard, the basketball team went 0–1952/53. An amazing statistic on which I rest my case. It is true we did not have a home court for basketball that year and had to play all our games on the road—the old gym was being torn down. I have no such excuse for my batting average the year before; it must have driven Fessor nuts to keep starting me with my zero average. Fessor was Richard Fayssoux, Athletic Director and head coach of the football, baseball, and basketball teams for over fifty years. I was nicknamed Goose (for Goose Egg) and lived up to the name until the last game of the season, against Hendersonville, a huge high school with over a thousand students. We were totally outclassed except for Bill Samford and Tudor Hall, two marvelous pitchers. Somehow toward the end of the game—tight because of the smoke our guys were throwing—I came up and got my first hit of the season, ended up on second base, and eventually scored either the tying or winning run, I cannot remember which now. Where else but at a place like Christ School could such a thing happen? Even the girl I was dating—from Saint-Genevieve-of-the-Pines—was there to see it. Of such things are careers made. The next year I batted over .300, just having needed that first hit.

The detail—something more luminous than an incident, something that is part of the true fabric of things—concerns the old gym, the shake-sided, dilapidated wooden structure that has been replaced twice since my days there. Behind it, overlooking the football field, was where we were allowed to smoke, if we were sixteen and had smoking permission. Pipes only. It was deep autumn or winter before I got my permission and I remember going out there after supper, in the dark, jacket turned up against the cold wind, and joining something I somehow knew was bigger than I could ever be, even though I was finally a part of it. I suppose what I was joining was Growing Up, though at the time I thought it apotheosizic. The three C's had started me on my way, but a smoking permit and the after-supper pipe (even though my head actually did spin) was the final event making me at last a true member of the school. How important that was to me, even to this day, I cannot quite express. Acceptance, as we all know, is everything at sixteen. I do not know how all this magic was worked through the windy, stolen moments behind the old-old gym, but I know it was. It was 1951 remember, a macho time in America and at Christ School: duck-tail haircuts, fourteen-inch pegged pants with welt seams and dual downs in back. Double Windsor knots, Mr. B collars. Lungsful of smoke. We were just trying to find out who we were—something no one can tell you, not even your memory. Especially your memory, that self-serving figment of someone you no longer even recognize or should even listen to.

When I think of the people at Christ School, I think first, always, of Mr. Dave, who made our classrooms so intense. I remember one big mistake I made—I took a Third Form history course my Sixth Form year. It was of course a breeze—until Mr. Dave took it over for a couple of weeks when the regular instructor, Mr. Hall, was sick. I got every question every day. Fortunately, I had a study hall the period before class, so I was able to memorize the lessons. Every day I memorized all the reading, since I would have to give it back to him word-for-word. To say that Mr. Dave got our attention is an understatement. He was also my trigonometry instructor, a course I had to pass to graduate. To say I understood nothing at all about the subject would also be an understatement. I needed a score of 66 and ⅔rds on my final exam to get out. As it happened, that was my precise score, and it was not until years later that I realized what a nice gift Mr. Dave had given me.

Mr. Dave, a name to conjure with. You never knew where he would turn up. I was convinced he had some kind of night vision, like a cat. He would appear out of the darkness, the coal of his cigarette like a small red eye, seeking out iniquity. And then disappear. In the daylight hours he was always squinting, especially with his right eye, avoiding the smoke from the ever-present cigarette stuck in the right corner of his mouth. (Maybe it was not "everpresent"; perhaps I think this because of our fixation on smoking—especially on cigarettes, which were totally taboo.) With a two-day growth of beard and the scowl of concentration on his face as he tried to find Sid, the handyman, or get the coal cars unloaded, or get to class, or get what was broken fixed, or what was wrong righted—a teacher's suicide, a student's girlfriend's pregnancy, a drunk and disorderly in Fourth Cottage—Mr. Dave seemed invariably on the move. Everything bent a little when he passed.

The Man was everywhere, imperturbable if he had to be, otherwise if he had to be. The school seemed to operate out of his body. Nothing happened without him—each meal, each meeting, each church service, and, if you were not careful, each illicit thing you were right on the verge of doing, just as you started doing it. There was The Man. Never have I felt such presence, such all-encompassing presence and power, since then—except possibly in the Sistine Chapel in Rome in 1959. Mr. Dave, as they used to say, was something else, and I treasure his memory. No matter what, he always met you halfway. In my case, of course, he came two-thirds of the way. Which brings me back to where I started.

What was I taking with me as I walked down those sun-drenched stone steps that morning in 1953, besides a stunning insensitivity to style and fashion, a diploma, an addiction to tobacco? The usual response is a Big Word, a Fundamental Value—Truth, Honesty, Integrity, Determination, Et cetera. Was I, for instance, determined to become a writer when I left? Probably not (but if I had been, it would have been because of my mother, not the school). As I remember, I was determined mostly just to get to Myrtle Beach for a week. Still, Mr. McCullough and Mr. Hale, my two English teachers, did nothing to hinder the writing possibility. Did my affinity for the spiritual side of things come from my days at Christ

School? Probably not, but it certainly was not hindered there. Again, my earlier upbringing is probably more important. Did my love of country music come from my days at Christ School? Actually yes, thanks to two friends—Bill Covin and Clem Webb. So Merle Travis and Hank Snow, plus an easy first year in college, where we repeated all my Sixth Form courses, was what I was taking with me into the Country of No Sweat. And one more thing. An abiding affection, a True Affection, if you will. For whatever reason, or reasons, I loved my two years there when I left. Everything about it, except for breakfast. All those biscuits!

Interlude

When tears come down like falling rain,
You'll toss around and call my name.
But sleep won't come the whole night through,
Your cheating heart will tell on you.

The song was usually into its second verse by the time we had been fully and oh-so-painfully awakened. Every morning, from the café juke box underneath the rooms we had rented for the week. Hank Williams and "Your Cheating Heart." Every morning well before 7:00 A.M., the same song, the same heat, the same taste of Myrtle Beach sand-dune grit in our mouths. I cannot remember just how many of us there were in that little apartment facing the beach, over the main road, over the café: all I know is that, as in the Rhymer's Club in turn-of-the-century London, there were too many. Sleeping on couches, beds, chairs, the floor, and occasionally in the bathroom, we had come down from the mountain for a week. Mostly to get drunk, as I recall. Down the chapel steps, a quick kiss and handshake for the beaming, apprehensive parents, into a couple of cars and then, So Long, Oolong: Henderson-ville, Flat Rock, the Saluda Grade, Spartanburg, Columbia, zoom . . . Jose Stuntz, Chip Hartenstein, Tommy Kirkland, Tudor Hall, Cutler Ham, Mac Hines, Jerry Knight, Bubba Tyler, Charlie Dameron . . . zoom. . . .

Well, sort of. By now, of course, that trip and that week and those people exist in another place—a place, as Paul Bowles intimates, that is so "other" it has stopped belonging to us and who we were and has become a zone, a region south of the past that lies at the edge of a mythic expanse of light, and which we more often talk of and then turn away from than we journey through. Who knows what we did: we came, we saw, we threw up, a perfectly sane and surgical battle plan to a seventeen-year-old boy, thorough idiocy to a fifty-five-year-old man as he stares out from the fort onto that hard plain, the sound of his heart beating more often arrhythmically than not, the sound of his breathing noticeably more noticeable than before. Who can remember? But the names remain, several of them candidates for the Great Names Hall of Fame—Lycurgus Cutler Ham, Huger Tudor Hall, Jose Stuntz—and the one song remains, forever associated with headaches, a queasy stomach, and an uncontrollable desire to lie down somewhere and go to sleep. Stuntz, Hartenstein, and Hall were famous in our school for a Christmas trip to Havana. All three came back with the clap, not to mention irresistible stories about naked female dancers picking up quarters with no hands, no feet, no teeth; stories about the amazing, pre-Columbian, ur-sized male members on display in the next floor show.

So we sat around Myrtle Beach and drank Cuba Libres all day—or as much of all day as we were able, probably about an hour. After getting badly sunburned on the first day, we had to avoid the beach or appear fully clothed, neither of which was conducive to meeting girls. But that was just as well; despite our stories and our imaginations, most of us were terrified by the mere thought of meeting strange girls. So we sat on the beach with our clothes on, telling ourselves what a great time we were having, praying that nothing more substantial, female-persuasion-wise, would have to happen.

Every night we would go to the dance rink, an outdoor, wooden, decklike affair by the water, and watch the college students dance to "Shake, Rattle and Roll," the big tune. After having spent countless hours bopping in practice back at school—left hand on the post of the double-decker bunk, right hand on our waists, back and shuffle, let-loose-and-pivot, up-on-the-toes, knees-together-boogie, drop-and-spin—we were ready for the big time. Or so we thought. Oh, we could have wailed—for sure with a bedpost to hang onto—but the girls were all so *old*, and the guys were all so *big*. And both were all so *unknown*. One time I did make a move. One time. After several evenings of standing around, trying to work up the gumption, I finally cut in on one girl. Both she and her partner looked at me as though I had brought them a dead dachshund to examine, then turned away.

My most vivid recollection of that entire week is the arrival of a 1954 Mercury hardtop convertible. We must have been sitting on the balcony looking out at the afternoon when it came down the road, very slowly, wanting to be looked at. Deeply into cars, we yelled at the driver, shouting out questions. He stopped, and we got to check out the first of the year's new cars. Here was something that *really* mattered. I remember remarking about the taillights, something about their new shape and something about how much better looking they were than those of the '53s. Serious conversation. Then the driver got back in and pulled back onto the highway. Slowly, very slowly, for full effect. I remember the taillights lighting up when he put on his brakes down the road. So red. So big and so red.

2. *The Kingsport Times-News*

One particularly warm evening in, I think, September of 1959, after supper and a solitary liter of wine, I was wandering through the back streets of Rome, around the Pantheon, and suddenly found myself in Piazza Colonna, in front of the House of Deputies. Off to my right I began to hear a familiar sound over the zip and spurt of Fiats and Vespas: the faint but unmistakable roll of a printing press. Approaching, I saw a large sign, "Il Popolo," on the side of a building. Light was coming out of a barred basement window, and I could see newsprint like a swift Mobius strip pathwaying out of sight. Outside the window, at the edge of the piazza, between the parked cars and the window light, reading fresh copy and wearing a newsprint watchcap, one of the pressmen sat in a cane chair, smoking. Having just the perfect amount of Frascati under my belt, I engaged him in conversation—in my Italian still fresh from a course at the Army Language School in Monterey, California—about my glory days in the newspaper game. Like all Italians I met in those days, he indulged me, offered me a smoke (but took one of my American, PX ones), and pretended that what a slightly drunk twenty-four-year-old American had to say about the romantic aspects of a job that probably had whittled his own life down to a stob was of interest. We passed, for my part, a pleasant hour together before I grained out into the darkness back toward the Pantheon and the bars of Piazza Navona. Bless him, whoever he was, kind and indulgent to callow youth.

I was talking about the three months I had spent working on my hometown paper in the summer of 1953, six years earlier, cleverly disguised to myself as a newspaperman. I worked the nightside for the *Kingsport News*—first as a backup and then as police reporter for the morning paper. The title "police reporter" is of course misleading, though at the time I considered it appropriately romantic and fitting. What the job required was checking the police blotter each evening; I found drunks and an occasional drowning, hit-and-run, or shooting. Most of the regular staffers worked the dayside. I was part of the downsized, nighttime holding crew, midnight's minions. Best job I ever had.

It began rather ominously. I was asked, my first afternoon there, to type something, and I said, "Type?" They said, "What?" And I said, "I can't. I don't know how." Imagine getting a summer job at a newspaper and not being able to type! So they said, "Start learning." And, for the next few days, I did; I typed, memorizing the keyboard. To this day I type with the three-finger style I taught myself there.

"There" was the newsroom on the second floor of a downtown brick building: two windows in front overlooking the street, the back giving onto the press room, where the linotype operators worked, which in turn gave way to the room containing the printing presses themselves. This was before

13

air-conditioning, before aluminum cans. Coca-Cola came in six-ounce green bottles, as God intended. I worked through many six-Coke nights that July and August, a nickel a pop from the machine. The newsroom itself, as I have mentioned, was staffed by remarkably few people: a night managing editor, Rudy Burke; a sports editor, Jack Kizer; a photographer, Lyle Byland; and a police reporter, me, "Chuck" Wright. I am sure they must have had a couple of real reporters, people who actually knew what they were doing, people who actually knew how to type, but naturally I do not remember them: memory's star is the Great Me. But I remember Janice Vaughn, my dayside counterpart on the woman's page. She was a sophomore from Mt. Holyoke College, a gorgeous and unapproachable older woman.

Boy Reporter: First Story

End of June. An accident at Cherokee Lake. The Boy Reporter is given the story and must find out: Who, What, When, Why, Where, and How.

> *Who:* subject unremembered.
> *What:* a drowning. The Boy Reporter got that right on the first telephone call to the police station.
> *When:* the Boy Reporter forgot to ask, so that was the first callback.
> *Why:* the Boy Reporter forgot to ask, so that was the second callback.
> *Where:* the Boy Reporter forgot to ask, so that was the third callback.
> *How:* the Boy Reporter forgot to ask, so that was the fourth callback.

Four callbacks to the same policeman! That is how the Boy Reporter learned the basics, meanwhile suffering acute and un-run-away-fromable embarrassment. But apparently I got enough of it together to make a readable piece, as, the next morning, there on the front page was the story, such as it was, with the byline: *By Chuck Wright, Times-News Staff Writer.* Nothing since has ever been so beguiling in print to me.

Boy Reporter: The Challenge

Night editor Rudy Burke—the Boy Reporter's ever kind, gentle, and helpful mentor—was of course "working on a novel." He was also, at least that summer, something of a drinker, and one evening he drank a lot. He came in drinking and would have left drinking had he left walking. It took a while for the rest of us to understand what was going on. But by about 9:00 P.M., we were beginning to catch on. When Lyle Byland came in from a shoot, he allowed as how Rudy was not long for our company and wondered where the bottle was. By the time Lyle found the empty under some stuff in Rudy's drawer, Rudy had already taken himself away by putting his head down on his desk, as he must have done long before in kindergarten, and going to sleep. Deep sleep.

Right after Lyle and I got back from taking Rudy home—his wife met us at the door in her bathrobe, but nothing much was said, there not being much to say—they turned to the Boy Reporter and said: Well, you've got to put the paper to bed now. What! Icicles, from stomach to colon: I've only just learned to type, and now I've got to be the editor? On Rudy's desk was the dummy for next morning's front page, half-blocked-out already and crinkled and smudged from his nap. They gave me a ruler. Someone said something about measuring the spaces for the cuts (the photographs); someone else said something about heads (headlines), column widths, and cutlines. Oh my. Time for the Boy Reporter to spring into action; time for the miraculous transformation. Cameras were rolling; it was Action City. Alas, the Boy Reporter resembled Jimmy Olsen more than Clark Kent, much less Superman. He tried, he really tried, but no sight was ever more welcome to his eyes than that of the Sports Editor, stumping up the stairs like Winnie-the-Pooh on his gimp leg, back from covering another dismal Class D, Kingsport Cherokees baseball game. To him, the front page was no more of a challenge than the sports page, which he plotted, measured, and graphed every night. Saved from disaster, the Boy Reporter leaned back, wiped the sweat from his brow, and watched Jack pound out his own column and put his own section to bed; watched Lyle

15

slip out the back way when everything was under control, probably off to the Moose or the Elk's Club; watched the linotype operators setting the type; and finally watched the white stairs of the moving paper climbing and settling into cut stacks. At last I watched the lights in the newsroom go out on the only edition of a newspaper I ever had a hand, however small and pink, in editing.

Boy Reporter: The Movie (Stills)

Lyle hung out in the darkroom, and since he was the easiest, freest, loosest, hippest character at the paper—just the "ests" I too wanted to be—I hung out in the darkroom as much as possible myself. Lyle was a character straight out of *The Front Page,* Ben Hecht's famous play: he carried a Speed-Graphic camera, was a sloppy dresser, drank a little all the time, and had a "gruff exterior and a heart of gold." At least to me he had those two attributes, and that was all I cared about. He took me, as the saying goes, under his wing, a wing I found to be slick and dark and exciting.

As the staff photographer, he was out much more than in, which was certainly all right with him. But because his pictures were mostly human interest or architectural, we seldom, if ever, worked together: the car crash shots were done solo and the stories written up from the police reports, for instance. So most of my exposure to him was in the darkroom— or the newsroom, where he would walk in saying deliciously outrageous things about the world in general and the *Times-News* and Kingsport in particular. Back in the darkroom he would get his chemistry going, both for the photos and for himself. The pint bottle was always near to hand, either in his pocket or in a handy drawer. But he never went over the line at work. That darkroom is where I was initiated into the joys of "nipping," little quick pulls washed down with Coke. It was where Lyle disabused me of the notion I had about continuing in newspaper work and not going to college. It was where, in the almost-dark, I began to see the faint outlines of the real world. It was where, at seventeen, I went for sustenance and was never let down, a place, as time went on, harder and harder to come by, a place, nowadays, cut into a light section and a dark section, where the curved shadow of the past rises through it. I will always see him with his sleeves rolled up, reaching me the half-empty bottle through the querulous glow of the safelight: "Here, kid, this'll take care of what ails you." It would not, of course, but the gesture did. God rest him all road ever he offended.

Boy Reporter: The Supper

Summers in Kingsport are a lot like summers elsewhere in the South: hot as hell. Each night I would eat my supper—a sandwich—in the front seat of a '52 Oldsmobile I had driven to work and parked on Center Street. For some reason I always left the sandwich, in its brown paper bag, in the car, on the front seat. By the time I got to it around 7:00 P.M., it had been blasted by the heat into an unimaginable limpitude, the lettuce hot to the touch, bread sagged and sogged, the whole affair untoothsome and unrelieved. I sat in the front seat of my car, ate my sandwich, drank my Coke, and read. It was the reading that was the important thing. I wish I could say this was the time I discovered the Classics, that *The Iliad* and *The Odyssey* are alive to me today because of those heat-defeated sandwich suppers in the summer of 1953. The fact is I read comic books—comic books and the novels of William Faulkner. I read most of Faulkner that summer. And a lot of comic books. One evening I remember finishing *As I Lay Dying* and then going up to the corner of State and Center Streets to ask the man-in-the-street what he thought about the Korean War ending that day. Faulkner should have inspired my best story, but he did not: my questions were no better, and the answers they elicited no better, than what we see on television today: inarticulate, intrusive, and stupid. Maybe if it had been a comic book supper I would have been more in synch and less intimidated. To this day I cannot smell bread or lettuce left out in the sun too long without that '52 Olds rising through the deeps to float in my mind's eye, with Flem Snopes and Wall Street Panic Snopes sitting in the front seat. Good grub.

Boy Reporter: The Off Hours

He played golf. He did not write stories, he did not write poems, he did not read books (except more Faulkner, when it rained). He just played golf. He did not hang around "colorful characters," he did not have a secret "old hat" he went to visit and talk to. He just played golf. No Possum, No Sop, No Taters. Just golf.

And in September, heeding Lyle's advice and his parents' expectations, he quit his job and his adolescence and went away to college, where he drank some beer, read a few books, played some golf, and never again wrote another news story. Not ever. Not to this very day. Still the best job he ever had.

Epilogue

I do not know what any of this has to do with the fact that some years later I began writing poems. I also do not know what any of this has to do with being Southern, other than that each of the three occasions happened in a Southern state—North Carolina, South Carolina, and Tennessee. None of the clichés and received "rites of passage" are necessarily indigenous to the South, though they are that too: all of them could have happened—God forbid—in New Jersey as well.

Thinking about the past is inherently sentimental—one always wishes things had been more of the same, less of the same, or partially or altogether otherwise, if only because we somehow believe the past, our past, still cares for us, as we care for it. This differs it from thinking about the desert, which we know does not care anything about anyone, anyway, or anyhow. One likes to think that the eye one casts on things above and below is the eye the desert casts—cold, hard, and unencumbered by time and events. Alas. The twin cataracts of desire and sadness all too often filter and realign the view. Probably just as well. The contour map of the past, with its transverse mercator projections, is the toughest terrain there is. To visit it seriously is literally to take your life in your hands. I remember once, some years ago . . .

Improvisations

With Father Hopkins on Lake Como

—4 June / Rereading in Hopkins' *Journals* yesterday: it's his reverence that strikes you, reverence for the minutiae as well as the miraculous, in their combinations as well as their separateness. Description, exactitude: a photo-realism from the insect to infinity. The spiritual eye that sees God's fingerprint and face on everything. And to look on something hard enough, that hard, is to change it.

Rain today, little apocalypses in the water beads mirroring the white, blank sky on broad leaves circling the goldfish pond. Downlake, cloud-curtain and mist-curtain obscure the mountains. White ferries appear and disappear like messengers far below from another country. The water beads explode and reform. How easily worlds come and go.

After you've been here long enough, Jim Barnes says, the blackbirds begin to whistle, in their ubiquitous but intermittent song, "prego," "prego."

They've cut the long grass in the olive orchard that spills down the deep slope below the main building, the Villa Serbelloni, to the lake. From above, the trees themselves appear shorn and reduced, as if their limbs, too, had been cut back. The trees in the adjoining, uncut field seem still full and olivesque; the ones in the field I just walked through, on the other hand, seem flattened, like hair wet from rain.

I was walking to the abandoned monastery, called locally "I Frati," The Monks, or The Brothers, where I have a room in the afternoons to work in. The monastery was built in the early 1600s by one of the Sfondrati, early owners of the property: when one of his sons wanted to become a priest, rather than have him leave home, the Duke built him a monastery of his own. Outside the window in front of my desk, a corner of the faded red tile and red plaster building cuts wedge-shaped, like a Giorgio Morandi painting, across the view. Beyond it are some cherry trees and olive trees and five rows of grape vines. Beyond that is a pine tree and then the lake. Beyond that the mountain above Varenna across the water, mist-bothered today and unfocused. Seagulls, crows, hawks, pigeons, sparrows, blackbirds, and various other feathered fellows rip in and out of the painting from time to time. Higher up, swallows freelance among the thermals. Here's one (a blackbird) on the roof tile saying "dunque," "dunque."

—6 June / Rain again. Steady rain. Uninterruptible strings. If we had a woof to cross with this warp, we would have a crystal curtain endlessly falling across the landscape, rain cloth collapsing in huge, invisible folds beneath the olive trees and the hemlocks. In the frog pond outside the window (this window in my other studio—I have two, one in the old monastery down the hill, in the afternoons, the other up the hill, in the mornings, a converted gazebo where the woods begin), the drops bulls-eye and blister the surface. The blisters form along the waterskin, drift momentarily toward the lilies, then break and vanish in tiny circles.* The lilies, open and yellow two days ago, stay half-closed and hunched beneath the incessant pressure from the head-taps of the rain beads.

Suddenly, after lunch, the rain stopped. Fifteen minutes later the sun was out and we all stepped onto the terrace, after three continuous days of downpour, as though we were stepping off the Ark. That branch of Lake Como that runs back toward Lecco was cleansed and accessible as I had never seen it in almost two weeks—small towns began to pile up on the

---

*There has to be a certain rhyme to the rainfall, a certain velocity, before the blisters can form—too little rain and the force isn't enough to bubble the surface, too much and they're destroyed, either before or during formation. Like everything else in this world, they have their own metrics, their own rhythms of being.

shoresides and mountainsides, red roof after red roof until the lake bent under the stern stone of the mountain, blue sky like a Chinese glaze seeped at all the corners of things.

Below, in the cloister yard, 5:30 sunshine fierce and finite, pushing down on the eyelids, coating the skin, two-thirds of the yard in shadow, shadow that gives the walls their color back, a yellowish Tuscan dun-orange. The part in sun is lighter, as though rinsed over and over to rid it of something. In the church, Peter is playing the oboe, winding North African sounds that circle and loop. Warrior ants forage and circulate over the flat stones in the courtyard, singly, each on his own mission. One never sees them in groups or pairs. If they are centaurs, the dragon hangs on the sunny walls, or crouches in the sunny corners, or rises immobile and enormous on the hard, rocky plain of the paving stones, waiting for some invisible thing. The ants let him loom as they scurry under the towering overgrowth of the yellow-topped flower weeds and the dandelion groves and the understory of clover and mustard grass. Dog soldiers, lone wolfscouts ceaselessly on the move. They meet and exchange a word or two, then break and are off again. The stone-plain and weed-forest are both alive with them. And here's a lizard down from the wall. In jerks and false starts he spurts and halts. Ants go over his tail and under his nose. Green as a piece of water, his body rises and falls, then streaks in one motion back toward the ivy and out of sight. The ants keep checking the territory.

Back upstairs, the windows open, afternoon sun on the lake and gray stone mountains, lake green as a lizard, light clear as water through glass. Surely the world is charged with the grandeur of God. At least from time to time.

—7 June / In the cloister courtyard, 11 o'clock in the morning. Each wall surrounding the inner yard is slightly different: west wall has six arches into the passageway that runs along all four sides of the cloister. There are two cells on the west side. The south has five arches and three cells, the east no arches but a door and two windows and thus has walled in the passageway—four cells. The north wall has five arches and no cells as it is the south side of the church. There is, of course, an upper passageway that's windowed, not arched, above the ground floor. In the courtyard itself, four cedar topiaries, one at each corner, four little boxwood diamonds enclosing them. In the center of the yard, a circle of boxwood containing a large stone urn, chipped and shaped by hand, very crude, very functional, and very beautiful. Red poppies grow in the circle. Yellow button-top weeds and yellow dandelions grow in the spaces between the paving stones, somewhat lighter in color than the walls, but not incompatible. Generations have walked to the urn, and walked back, have walked the quadrangle under the arches, the stone steps and paving stones. But none does now. Only the maintenance supervisor, whose office is in the east wing, unbalances the solitude now and then. Down here, where the heart of the order tapped out its daily routine, every door is locked but one. Just now, a hawk sailed over toward the lake, mewling and meowing like a cat. The swallows shrieked and subsided, their shadows descending and climbing the walls as they drag the air for food. A truck pulls up the hill, a Weed-Eater coughs and stops in the adjoining field. Quietness . . . Stillness . . . Cheep of baby swallows somewhere out of sight. Weeds bow in the small breeze. Poppies, hooded and cowled, nod in their noontime doze. Lisp and swish of a swallow's wing. Have trod, have trod . . .

The only unlocked door leads to the crypt. Twenty walled-in burial slots in the walls, nine each on two sides and two in the north wall. On the south wall, the only window has a painting, very faded, of a monk holding the Baby Jesus on his lap over it. Under the window, a small stone altar, just large enough to hold the bodies that were lowered from the church above through the hole—now sealed over—in the ceiling a short while before entombment. Each of the twenty tombs is sealed by a slab of hand-hewn, gray stone, the same stone the mountains around here are made of, the same stone the stairs, the lintels, the doorjambs, the windowsills and archway sills are made of. At the top of each slab, a skull and crossbones looks out, a cross on top of the skull, each painted there, not enfrescoed. Most of the information painted below the skulls has eroded from dampness, but several dates can still be

read—1761, 1790, 18-something—and a name or two—
Giovanni da Bellano is one—and one anonymous tomb is
legible: Un Pellegrino da Lecco (A Pilgrim from Lecco). One
tomb, on the right in the north wall, differs from all the rest—
it has a skeleton painted on the slab. And that's all. They
recked his rod.

—8 June / Deluge. Whitecaps like ocean waves breaking on a
beach ride down the lake under a north wind. Rain almost
solid in its intent and descent. Lightning behind the cloud and
shifting mist-mass like klieg lights shot on and off behind
gauze draperies. Tremendous and rolling claps from the
thunder-throne. One hour south of here the World Cup soc-
cer tournament begins today. Right where the storm rolls,
down the lake, the battle, as Miss Bishop said, now in another
part of the field. Justin Kaplan left this morning. Big rip in
the social fabric. Yesterday at lunch he told the story of two
tanks, one Israeli, one Egyptian, that collided during a battle
in the desert during the Six Day War. The Egyptian driver
climbed out with his hands over his head, repeating, "I surren-
der, I surrender." The Israeli climbed out of his tank at the
same time, rubbing the back of his neck and muttering, "Oi,
whiplash."

Intense green stretch marks over the lakeskin where the
tide currents slide just under the surface after a storm. One of
a series of storms that has tumbled and fulminated out of the
Alps behind us. A black pigeon is strolling in the rain along
the roof tiles outside the window, now scruffily getting wetter
on the ridge line of the building, jerking and bobbing his head
as though the sun were out. Here comes the hard stuff again.
And there he goes. GMH's death day, 101 years ago.

—12 June / False neon of afternoon, crow in the Chinese pine
bare-branched at lake's edge, seagull and pigeon skim over
greencap and whitecap. Inside, in the cloister yard, three sun-
dials shadow the hour against the church wall's south side.
The hour shadows me. I shadow a lizard upside-down on the
same wall. His shadow shadows the world.

Along the gray stone walls going down to the village, tiny

young ferns have appeared, growing out of the moss and concrete, like clusters of tangled, miniature green starfish arms jutting from the stones.

—14 June / Reading through the journals, one is constantly struck by the faith GMH has, and the absolute certainty of that faith: that when he decides to describe something—a leaf, a wave or series of waves, a bird, a landscape sweep—minutely or particularly, he is able to transcend it, through language, and enter whatever it is he is describing; that the inscape is knowable and tactile through language. That the heart of the mystery, the pulse at the very unspeakable center of being, is apprehensible through writing about it. Thus the lovingly, intricately laid down musical strings of language. One no longer believes this is possible. One more often now knows that the only answer to inscape is silence. How marvelous, however, to see how the world once seemed, how Adamic it all was before the word and the world became separate. And the Word and the world became separate.

Crow shadows climb the evergreens outside the window, tiny, quick black crosses up, up and dissolve as the birds circle and plane above the spruce and pine woods. Like moving imprints of the Unholy Ghost, they rise and vanish so rapidly one is tempted to think one didn't see them. But one did. One always has . . .

—15 June / GMH has style, style to burn, onto-theological style. It is one of the several reasons he continues to haunt us, both in his poems and in his prose. He has, in fact, great style. Great style is transcendence and flash. It is that moment of exscalation, that moment when the light of recognition and understanding, the phosphorous-flare of perception renatures a thing. You find the burn and you feed it. There is, as Hopkins said, the dearest freshness deep down things. True style exfoliates this into the sudden glare of awareness. GMH's inscape, Joyce's epiphany, Cézanne's simultaneous presentation are all moments of exscalation. Great style is like that, linked moments of exscalation down the page—fluid, not static and insular, the after-aura of rediscovery flooding the thing in question. I'm talking about poems here—the after-aura spreading and interlocking, a retreating radiance highlighting language and its excavations of new combinations and new geographies.

—16 June / Going down to the monastery from the Villa, you go through the olive orchard. A path of flat stones, approximately two foot square each (although they aren't square), paving stones, is set in the ground from the top to the bottom of the orchard. At the beginning of the descent, as though an offering stone among the more pedestrian and utilitarian ones, is a small, dark gray, grainy rectangular stone. It has a carving—more precisely, a bas-relief—engraved in it, now worn almost smooth. Still visible, however. Probably part of a frieze on some building, or even a cemetery decoration. It resembles—the figure—something, I fancy, of Gwan Yin, the Chinese goddess often depicted with flowing drapery falling away from her. Her body, in the Italian sunlight and rain, sentinel of the track through the sacred olive grove, each season growing smaller and less defined, her amphora-like figure so still, so still this morning in the first summer day-haze. Our Lady of the Olives.

Interesting to me that GMH set, or said he set, only two of his own poems to music—"Hurrahing in Harvest" and "Spring and Fall"—from a total of some twenty-seven settings there are either music for or mention of, given the aggressive "musical" base he advertised as grounding his poems. Perhaps they were written for instruments that don't exist yet. Or have been forgotten. I would love to have heard Billie Holliday sing "Spelt from Sibyl's Leaves." Uh huh . . .

As for poetry and speech and meaning: one knew this already, but it's interesting to see it in writing (in a little piece entitled "Poetry and Verse")—"Poetry is . . . speech framed to be heard for its own sake and interest even over and above its interest of meaning . . . (Poetry is in fact speech only employed to carry the inscape of speech for the inscape's sake—and therefore the inscape must be dwelt on)."

Seagulls drifting over, backlit by the sun—their wings translucent, or wing back-feathers translucent, as they balance and right themselves over the hemlocks and evergreen topiary. Strangely unplaced, their black wing-centers trailed by pinions flamed out like a shining, they circle, lazy boomerangs, in their fiery gyres.

—17 June / I've watched a lizard patrol the sunny edge of a boxwood hedge for about forty-five minutes now. Back and forth, never venturing into the shadow, occasionally stopping suddenly to rub, vigorously, his forelegs against the ground. Is he hunting? He never, that I could see, found anything. Is he ranging his territory? What is it that lizards do, little sticks, little swift sticks, belly to the ground, taking the sun this Sunday? They hold the world together, that's what.

—18 June / Excursion yesterday to the upper end of the lake to see two churches, one the Abbazia at Piona and the other S. Maria del Tiglio in Gravedona. The Abbazia—a seminary abbey—is eleventh century, but modernized into indiscrimination. On the grounds, behind the church, the Cistercian brothers have built a miniature replica of the grotto at Lourdes. On Sunday, as yesterday was, crowds come to sit in the shade of the giant cypress in front of the shrine—a shrine, in fact, that consists of a bank of electric candles inside the fake grotto: insert a coin and a candle is turned on—all day. Families with the physically unfortunate member—a Downs Syndrome child, a legless and armless brother, a disturbed daughter—sit quietly, hoping, I suppose, for some magic radiation out of the mortar and stone. For the afflicted. Or, more probably, for themselves, to lighten the load. Has it come to this? Of course it has—it has always come to this . . . S. Maria del Tiglio was more authentically preserved. Also eleventh century, they solved the modernization problem by building a new church next door in the 1800s, thus avoiding the layering that has bastardized the Abbazia. In all, a disappointing trip; even the ice cream was mediocre as we waited for the hydrofoil to take us back down the lake.

Outside the window, in a fern clump, an almost perfect replica of the Janus face in the leaves' configuration. Or the Devil's visage. At the right time, in the right circumstances, I could declare a vision, etc., and set up shop. As it is, it is only the physical world, as it always does, trying to jump-start the imagination. The morning begins to settle itself across the lake, warm breast, bright wings.

—June, 1990 / Bellagio

Titleism

The resurgence of narrative, like old water in a clean tub, in current poetry is cause for alarm. The reinsistence on explanatory oddments and surface effects is both disappointing and deleterious. It is as though, in an age of flight, someone had reinvented the wagon. One group—too small to be called a school, too isolated to be called a movement—has become alarmed enough to create a counter current. Beyond Imagism, beyond Minimalism, Titleism, as the new discipline has come to be called, effectively combines the desired end result of both Zen meditation and Judeo-Christian transcendence. Essentially a spiritual exercise (as most great poetry tends to be), it thus eschews a manifesto, though it does lay out five tenets as dogma. These tenets are not descriptive, but prescriptive. If followed, they will eliminate 99 percent of the useless welter of bad narrative that impedes the way. Or, as they say, "One Titleist poem is worth a thousand words." The five are:

1. The proper title *is* the poem.
2. The less said the better.
3. Mum's the word.
4. Silence speaks for itself.
5. Less is more, nothing is less.

On these tenets hang all the poems and their prophets.

The Hydrosyllabic Foot

The hydrosyllabic foot runs uneasily through the lines of most free verse poems today. It is characterized, usually, by its tendency to flood and overrun its banks more often than it remains contained in its proper, and strength-giving, boundaries. Such propensity leads most free verse poems to exist, as it were, under water instead of under technical control. It makes writers think of check-offs and exits and unions instead of firmly established channels, networks of linguistic irrigation. The hydrosyllabic foot is, of course, endlessly expandable and impossible to define, yet has—perhaps because of this—a certain theoretical cachet because of its historical allusiveness. Naturally, everyone wants to claim it as his own. It has an amazing bonding propensity to the outward aspects of prose—discursiveness instead of concision, explanation instead of innuendo, a filling in of all the blanks instead of leaving a few empty to whet the imagination. In fact, the hydrosyllabic foot is not a foot at all in the real sense—that is to say in any quantitative, poetically operative way—but is an attitude. In 1915, Pound made the sentence the general unit of measure in *Cathay*. And since the sentence was almost always, in these translations, a self-contained line, he thus established the line, the individual line, as the unit of measure in subsequent free verse. The hydrosyllabic foot has extended that concept, making prose itself the unit of measure in most current free verse, becoming a slide rule without numbers, a compass without a stationary peg, a protractor without angles. It is, in the long run and the short, a crisis of faith. What started out as an attempt to loosen and include turns into a bad case of presbyopia, an inability to see with the inner eye and inability, extended, to hear with the inner ear. There has become no greater handicap in poetry. How amazing it is, really, that so many embrace its fluid and uncontrollable demands. The variable foot of William Carlos Williams had a golden ear behind it and a passion for change. The syntactical unit measure of Pound had a golden ear behind it and a rage for instruction and retrieval. The elastic foot of T. S. Eliot had a brilliant ear behind it and a passion for both history and advancement. And all three practitioners, of course, had a deep education in metrics and knew what they were leaving, and why. Still, the hydrosyllabic foot does have its seductions. For instance, one can step in it twice. And then some. For instance, its movements depend, apparently, on "breaks" in its line of progress rather than any interior coherence in the line being written. For instance, where it's going has little to do with how it gets there. A slippery poetic, many-headed, slipshod and any-gaited, a line for all landfalls.

Improvisations

The Poem as Journey

"I am writing to you from a far-off country," "I am writing to you from the end of the world," Henri Michaux, the French Surrealist poet, says. Precisely. Most, if not all, good poems come from that place, or those two places if they have become separated by intent or degree. Like the continents and like imagination, they started as one mass, but both have devolved to a movable attitude. Dante wrote from the Empyrean, a far-off country, indeed. Others write from next door, which often can be the end of the world.

So many journeys. So many destinations. Orpheus descending through the byways and back canals of the human body, Ulysses and Aeneas blown to and from all those lands and islands of the natural world, Dante and Leopardi arrowing in and out of the various heavens and the stars. And what is the ultimate resting place of all these peregrinations, the landscapes we travel through, the roads we go back and forth on, or the time it takes us to get there or fail to arrive?

"A journey is a fragment of hell," Bruce Chatwin says in *Songlines*. An inch or a thousand miles, I say, in whatever direction, up or down. But that's the road the good poem takes. Most everyone thinks it's the road that counts, that the

Delivered as the second Claudia Ortese Lecture in American Literature, May 14, 1992, L'Universitá Degli Studi di Firenze, Florence, Italy.

traveling is the point of the journey, both in life and in art. I
disagree. I think it's what's at road's end that is important, that
where the road leads is where the meaning is: it's not the
telling of the story that's important, it's what the story has to
tell. The telling is interesting, but the point is what's transcen-
dent. As a younger man, I thought that process was meaning.
I now know that meaning is meaning, and that journey's end
is the end of the journey, not some intermediate point—the
road to Campostela leads to Campostela, the road to Assisi
ends in Assisi, not at Gròpina.

Poems are not just *about* journeys, of course, they *are* jour-
neys—surreptitiously, silently, staying in one place the way
plants do. Like any organism, the good poem is a self-
contained adventure, both physically and metaphysically. What
Eihei Dogen, the Japanese Zen master, said about the plan-
tain in the century Dante was born can as well be said about
the good poem: "A plantain has earth, water, fire, wind,
emptiness, also mind, consciousness and wisdom as its roots,
stems, branches, and leaves, or as its flowers, fruits, colors
and forms. Accordingly, the plantain wears the autumn wind,
and is torn in the autumn wind. We know that it is pure and
clear and that not a single particle is excluded." If it lacks
these essential components, the plantain does not grow to its
fullest expectations. If the poem lacks them, it goes no-
where. Moribund and ill-equipped, it becomes a shell—
without the interior journey, the exterior one is impossible.
The true journey is a healthy plant; the true poem is the
same thing.

At the heart of every poem is a journey of discovery. Some-
thing is being found out. Often the discovery is merely
technical—architectural, metrical, or spatial—though, when
lucky, the technical revelation is not just "merely" but is an
uncovered new thing. Poetic structures sometimes end up in
that fortunate "field." New concepts of lineation often do as
well. From time to time the discovery is spiritual, a way of
looking at the world that affects the way we lead our lives, or
how we think of them. Poems that cause us to say, after having

read them, "Oh, that's nice," or "Ummm, not bad," do not participate in this voyage of discovery. No matter how new their paint job is, no matter how smart and crisp their sails, they never get out of the harbor. The journey belongs to others.

Two twentieth-century Italian poets—Dino Campana and Eugenio Montale—make an interesting comparison. Campana, who restlessly writes of almost nothing but journeys on foot, by sea, or all manner of transportation, to both spiritual and quotidian places, has a turbulent and frenzied surface to his poems, but underneath a Romantic standstill and stasis. Montale, on the other hand, whose poems have, for the most part, placid and one-place-at-a-time surfaces, underneath have a miraculous sense of voyage to previously undiscovered or forgotten states of being. Another famous twentieth-century poet, Giuseppe Ungaretti, in his minimalistic sensibility, also constantly carries us elsewhere. His two-word, two-line poem "Mattina"—"M'illumino / d'immenso"—says about all there is to say on the subject of epiphanic discovery (and is my favorite example of why translation is ultimately impossible). To finish off the parallelism, Pier Paolo Pasolini, whose movies were a constant exploration of both physical and psychic revelation—as were his novels—had to my way of thinking a very ordinary and unadventurous venture in his poems. His life, as we know, followed his novels and films, even to its abrupt, and sad, ending.

The imagination is, of course, the starter's pistol of all journeys. As Federico García Lorca, the great Spanish poet of the 1930s, has said, "it travels and transforms things, endowing them with their purest sense, and it identifies relations which had never been suspected. . . . Imagination is the first step, the foundation of all poetry." Inspiration, the dark twin and demiurge of imagination, can, he later counsels, send the traveler farther and deeper than imagination alone, creating a poetry where "a man more rapidly approaches the cutting edge that the philosopher and the mathematician turn away from in silence." That "cutting edge," where all true poems climb from and return to, is the edge where the void begins.

And it is inspiration, pure instinct, to which Lorca eventually pays the greater homage. Imagination is closely allied to intelligence and logic/reasoning. And intelligence, he said, "is often the enemy of the poet, because it limits too much, and it elevates the poet to a sharp-edged throne where he forgets that ants could eat him or that a great arsenic lobster could fall on his head." The journey is always into the unknown, into the mystery and darkness where great lobsters fall on our heads and great unseen wings graze our faces and vanish.

Back to Montale for a moment. Just about thirty years ago, I translated into English (American, really) a section of his poems "Lampi e Dediche" ("Flashes and Dedications") from his book *La bufera*. These little poems had such a profound effect on me that I then went on to translate the entire book—the first time, I might add, that the complete *La bufera* had been done in English. It has since, of course, become a mountain that many have climbed. However, my point here is with the short, diary-like section, "Lampi e Dediche." What first drew me to these poems was their strong, and strange, religious overtones. This is rare in Montale's work and, even here, it is not "religion" per se, but rather a peculiar sort of mysticism, little apocalypses, immense journeys in tight and loaded little packets.

The opening poem in the series, "Verso Siena," serves to show that God is a possibility, though how He is to be taken, and how Montale takes Him, we are never sure. This uncertainty gives the power of the unknown, the mystery, and the journey's end as an addition to the imagistic pyrotechnics in the poems themselves. The reader—after going through such other poems as "Sulla colonna più alta," "Incantesimo," and "Vento sulla mezzaluna"—knows he has traveled to a different universe indeed in things Montaliane, a universe almost completely comprised of nothingness (a familiar place at first). But this time nothingness is not all; there sometimes appear certain perceptions (*lampi*) that carry almost metaphysical overtones of faith.

Montale's world, as we know now, is a fascinating one, with a sense of time as a steady destroyer, of existence as entropy, an inevitable process of decay. But it is the added dimension found in "Lampi e Dediche" that gently alters that world, which hints of the changes that came later in *La bufera*, when the journey went down and down, deeper into the darker waters of personal history, and the century's history. *"O voi chi siete in piccioletta barca,"* as Ezra Pound had it from Dante. Out of my way. *Pista!*

And speaking of Uncle Ez, as Montale called him, and as he called himself on Italian radio, we have a fine example of someone who tried the ultimate journey in his work, a Dantean-Joycean voyage that ended up, by his own admission, shipwrecked on the rocks of history, prejudice, and Western culture in general, the very land's end he was headed for all along. Having had his epic—his non-narrative epic (which Montale said was a contradiction in terms)—progress *in periplum,* where the winds took it, and not on any preset, direct-narrative course, this is not surprising. But it remains one of the most spectacular and gorgeous literary wrecks, in English, of the century, and the lyrical songs that continue to rise from the wreckage, and the incredible music and visions of many of its parts continue to seduce us toward that same shore and those same shoals, a broken bundle of mirrors though they may be.

Having said that about Pound, let me say something else, something more personal about his work and its early effects on me. I have said this before in another place, but it bears repeating when we are speaking of journey and poetry, as it concerns the beginning of my own journey, without Ariadne's thread, into the maze. All first loves are ultimately sad. They begin in such light and splendor and end in darkness and disillusion. Later they are brought back up to shine again like discovered lost treasure from the old waters of indifference. My poetic first love was no different from this. And it was Ezra Pound.

I have written at some length, and almost continuously, for over thirty years about my first stay in Italy, which began in January, 1959. Such obsessive attempts at re-creation are some slight indications of the abiding effect the country and its culture, and my initial baptism by total immersion in it, had—and continues to have—on me.

My most momentous occasion, at least in what was to preoccupy me from then on, and what I still, as I once said, "waste my heart on," was a trip I took to Lake Garda from Verona, where I lived, and particularly to Sirmione, the peninsula at whose tip Catullus, the legend goes, had a villa, the ruins of which to this day stun the unwary foreign traveler when he comes upon them. I was such a traveler, clutching in one hand the *Selected Poems of Ezra Pound,* bought two years previously in New York City and still unread. My friend Harold Schimmel, with me in the army in Verona, had borrowed it in the first weeks of our friendship and had returned it with the admonition to read the poem "Blandula, Tenulla, Vagula," which was about the very spot I would be visiting. And so I did, the late March sun pouring through the olive trees, reflecting off their silver and quicksilver turns in the lake wind, the lake itself stretched out below me and into the distance, the pre-Alps above Riva cloud-shouldered and cloud-shadowed, the whole weight of history and literature suddenly dropping through the roof of my little world in one of those epiphanic flashes that one is fortunate enough to have in one's lifetime now and then if one is ready. I was ready. The continuous "desire to write" that I had had since high school had finally found its form—the lyric poem. The irresistible force had met a movable object. A week later Schimmel and I took off for a week's leave—down to Bologna, over *La Futa* and the Apennines, through Florence, Rome, Naples, and finally to Paestum in southern Italy—and my focus was set for the rest of my life, as hyperbolic as that might sound. I still have that little paperback book, and it still has the heavy, army-issue-paper slipcover on it that Harold made back in 1959. The number 1302 is written in ink on the cover, a number that means nothing to me.

But the book means something to me, and the poems meant something to me in my green time. One's personal poetic journey has to begin before the journey inside the poem can get under way.

And speaking of Verona, it was there, I think, that a girl I knew back in 1959 or 1960 said to me one afternoon, during the course of a courtship that went back and forth between Milano, where she lived, and Verona, where, as I say, I lived, *"Guarda,* Charles, *quando io faccio una cosa, io vado fino in fondo, sai." Ostrighetta!* I was a young guy then, and young guys just want to have fun. Fun for her meant something else, however. It meant, finally, *"andare fino in fondo."* She did, I didn't.

Such a course, *"Andare fino in fondo,"* was no fun for John Berryman, an American poet of a recent generation who did just that in both his life and his poems. The voyage to the bottom of the soul. He took it and his poems took it. It was tragic in his life and brilliantly redemptive in his art. It was just such a journey that a group of poets, called the Confessionals, all but one of them of the same generation, took: they were Berryman, Robert Lowell, Anne Sexton, W. D. Snodgrass, and Sylvia Plath. Delmore Schwartz and Randall Jarrell were peripheral members. Four of them committed suicide, two died young, and one, probably the originator of the kind of writing the group was known for, though not its most illustrious member, is still alive. Some journeys from the void know secret shortcuts, some have no return ticket.

Berryman and his alter egos, Henry and Mister Bones, dance the Dance of Death, that dark and monotonous soft-shoe, across the stage of *The Dream Songs,* a huge book of almost exclusively eighteen-line poems about the foibles, momentary triumphs, and endless vicissitudes of Henry as he shuffles inexorably off stage left to his predestined and preternatural doom. The entire enterprise is a kind of *commedia del l'arte* stage setting, the characters, especially Henry, rather like marionettes or puppets just waiting to collapse or to be pulled under at any moment. We are not disappointed. In brilliant set piece after brilliant set piece, the excruciating ritual is played out to its appointed end, Henry and Berryman himself, puppet and puppeteer, finally subsumed by the journey itself. Ars brevis, vita brevis est.

Franz Kafka, in one of his entries in *The Blue Octavo Notebooks,* writes: "Before setting foot in the Holy of Holies you must take off your shoes, yet not only your shoes, but everything; you must take off your travelling garments and lay down your luggage; and under that you must shed your nakedness and everything that hides beneath that, and then the core and the core of the core, then the remainder and then the residue and then even the glimmer of the undying fire. Only the fire itself is absorbed by the Holy of Holies and lets itself be absorbed by it; neither can resist the other." This is the kind of journey we are talking about. . . .

For many of us in our youth, Hart Crane was the ultimate American poetic icon. His poem "The Bridge" is second only to Pound's *Cantos* as the most spectacular and seductive failure of the twentieth century in American poetry. There is something irresistibly sexy and alluring about ambition and the failure of that ambition, especially if its scattered or gathered parts have a kind of glittering perfection, as those of both the *Cantos* and "The Bridge" do.

The wake of the SS *Orizaba* had hardly closed over Crane's body before his personal legend began to take shape. His literary one was not far behind. He had tried for the impossible in his poem—his great, shattered poem—a journey across time, history, and personal recognition that refused to redeem either him or literature and refused to come together—two lacks that mirrored the disconnections in his own life. The way out seemed the way in, and he took it. The verb "to voyage" is just as inaccessible and untranslatable in the heart as it is in the poem.

Hart Crane was unafraid in his literary ambitions. Many, of course, profess to be unafraid and are willing "to try anything." The vast majority of such people say and do such out of ignorance and foolhardiness. Crane did it out of talent, genius, and a vision, a vision that was not to be thwarted. True vision *is* journey. True vision is a bridge from here to there. Crane saw his road and set out on it. At its end was the end. Had he known that before he set out, I'm convinced he would have acted no differently. Genius must keep its appointments. We are still picking up and examining the dazzling flotsam and jetsam, just as we are from the *Cantos*. Hart Crane and

Ezra Pound, the two fallen angels in the American twentieth-century poetic firmament. How they shine and flare in their fiery arcs.

Does the journey currently seem shorter and less ambitious? Have the truly incredible occurrences of this century shrunk and shortened the reach of poets and poems? E. M. Cioran accuses Paul Valéry of corrupting generations of French poets, he and Stéphane Mallarmé, by their insistence that every poem be an exercise in the impossible, that every poem be a leap from a high wall by the poetic body. Rather like the famous photograph staged by the French artist Yves Klein, where he is shown in midair, stretched out, having just jumped from a high stone wall down to a Parisian stone street. We now know that the photograph is a collage and that, in actuality, there was a net beneath the original leap to catch him, now excised, with a cleverly added picture of the street creating the physical disaster he seems headed toward.

Indeed, most journeys are, perforce, of this kind in poems. And that's all right, I think. Otherwise the landscape and the history of literature would be strewn with bodies and maimed poems. Short journeys are not only acceptable, they are necessary to make the longer ones possible and legendary. Dante needed Lapo Gianni and Guido Cavalcanti. Montale needed Cesare Pavese and Salvatore Quasimodo. An inch or infinity, to the stars or to the *norceria,* through the thickets of the soul or the thickets of language, down the boulevards of the heart or the thoroughfares of technique. The journey remains the same in the good poem—it goes from point A to point B. Distance does make a difference and depth does make a difference, but vision is still vision, whatever its scope or manifestations.

Emily Dickinson was stationary. By that I mean her life was stationary. Her mind was a long-distance runner, unstill, never ceasing. Her imagination and inspiration were lightning-strikes and full of a great illumination. She sat in her room and the galaxy unrolled beneath her feet. She sat in her room and the garden and orchard outside her windows took on the ghostly garments of infinity. In her finest poems, and everywhere throughout her letters and the rest of her poetry, there has seldom before been such expansiveness in such small containers. Her poetry was an electron microscope trained on the infinite and the idea of God. Such distances under her fingertips! Inside the tube of the climbing rose, the River of Heaven flowed. Under the oak's throat, the broken ladder to Paradise waited for reassembly.

During the last ten years of her life she apparently seldom left her room, or at least the second story of her house. For most of her life she had been reclusive. Yet her poems are immense voyages into the unknowable. To leave she had to stay still, something Dino Campana was unable to accept, for instance, or was incapable of doing.

There was the famous white dress. There was the famous white flower. There was the famous "white election." And there was the famous last letter she wrote, the day before her death, to her two cousins, Louise and Fannie Norcross— "Little Cousins—Called back. Emily"—sounding almost as though she were an alien, some extraterrestrial who was here on a visit. She does seem "inhabited" in a way. Or perhaps she was Manichaean, a kind of Cathar whose chip of light was to begin its last, and longest, journey back to the original and unthinkable source of all light, leaving this darkness for good. Whatever, she remains one of the great lyric poets of all time. Sappho casts no shadow on her, her sherry-eyed opposite. . . .

Every journey is the same journey, and every journey is different. The journey in life, as the song says, is a lonesome valley. The journey in the poem runs toward higher ground, the ridgebacks and upper slopes, hilltop to mountaintop. The movement, in other words, tends to be upward. At least it has been that way for me.

The iconic book in my life, the work toward which all my work has aspired, is the *Confessions* by Saint Augustine. It is that kind of autobiography, in a more temporal—though no less spiritual—sense, I suppose, that my poems want to describe. Or to show their inability to describe. In either case, the journey is the same journey, even if the station reached is dramatically different. One goes where one is called.

The journey in the Chinese poem, which has also been of interest to my work, is otherwise. Where our Western movement, as I say, tends to be upward, the Chinese aim deliberately downward, at the earth, at the landscape and the tactile world and their tenuous place within it. It is a poetry of seeing, and their spiritual strength is in that seeing and in the things of this world they look at. And since they have no belief in a future world—as, say, Christians do—they love what they look at with a passion the Western tradition does not contain. Their sense of the permanence of the world is as strong as our sense of its transience.

It has been said that Buddhism has provided a spiritual basis for Chinese landscape poetry. One does sense the great interior Zen journey, that long and arduous trek to the still, quiet center of things, reflected in the description of landscape and in the patience and absolute faith of certain onlookers such as Cold Mountain (Han Shan) or Wang Wei. The poets and poems from the T'ang Dynasty (618–907) are generally accepted as being the finest examples of this, though the T'ang poets were using forms and song patterns, we now know, which were themselves up to four hundred years old, brought down from the time of the Han. If, as Gustave Flaubert said, the Good Lord does live in the detail, then these short poems which often centered upon the enduring problems of man's life can be said to be large spiritual voyages as the Chinese looked around themselves and told how it was to be here at this time, in this place, letting the waters of the River of Heaven slide over their heads and the waters of the Yangtze slide under their feet. The enormousness of the material world and all the roads that wind through the ten thousand things!

While it is not poetry but fiction, the writing of Ernest Hemingway has been very influential in my life. The book that I read as a young man and never quite got out of my system is *The Short Stories of Ernest Hemingway*. There is a purity of description, a purity of language at its most effective, that has always been seductive to me in his writing, and I find it—or found it so when I was younger—most prevalent in his stories. It is a purity of language in action that I have often aspired to in my poems.

Such stories, for example, as "A Clean, Well-Lighted Place," "Hills Like White Elephants," and "The Short Happy Life of Francis Macomber" seemed to me perfectly articulated and took the reader to a faraway place, an effortless journey of narrative and style. It is such a place I wanted my poems to have access to, and the roads that led there I wanted my poems to be able to travel. Especially the early, crystalline vignettes of *In Our Time*. Like Chinese poems, they gave a sense of the long journey through the possibilities of language, its exclusions as well as its inclusions. I thought they were "true" in the way Hemingway liked to use the word, and I loved them.

It's always been my contention that the shorter the distance, the harder the journey. By that I mean there is less time and less space to get said what has to be said. For that is the real journey after all—what you've got to say. We can metaphor and simile and weave intricate euphemisms till our pencils stub out of lead, but the fact remains that what you have to say is where you have to go. How you say it, of course, can grease the wheels and fuel the engine (here we go metaphoring again) and can sometimes actually be what you are talking about, but for the most part, you've got to say your way to seize the day. And the more condensed the poem is, the less maneuvering room there is, the stronger the message and the greater the journey is after the fact, which is where all real journeys start out. Dante is an example of this.

But there are contemporary poets who illustrate my point as well as Dante, including Jorie Graham, an American with significant connection to Italy. Jorie grew up in Rome and, in 1966, was a member of the army of students who came to help salvage books from the Arno's mud after the floods here. When I asked her to respond to my view of the journey in our poems, Jorie Graham replied in a letter, and gave the following explication. Her explanation helps make the case for that "journey of technique" I mentioned earlier. I want to present first her poem "San Sepolcro" and then what she says about the poem:

San Sepolcro

In this blue light
    I can take you there,
snow having made me
    a world of bone
seen through to. This
    is my house,

my section of Etruscan
    wall, my neighbor's
lemontrees, and, just below
    the lower church,
the airplane factory.
    A rooster

crows all day from mist
    outside the walls.
There's milk on the air,
    ice on the oily
lemonskins. How clean
    the mind is,

holy grave. It is this girl
    by Piero
della Francesca, unbuttoning
    her blue dress,
her mantle of weather,
    to go into

labor. Come, we can go in.
    It is before
the birth of god. No-one
    has risen yet
to the museums, to the assembly
    line—bodies

and wings—to the open air
    market. This is
what the living do: go in.
    It's a long way.

> And the dress keeps opening
>> from eternity
>
> to privacy, quickening.
>> Inside, at the heart,
> is tragedy, the present moment
>> forever stillborn,
> but going in, each breath
>> is a button
>
> coming undone, something terribly
>> nimble-fingered
> finding all of the stops.

If I consider "San Sepolcro," the journey seems especially a *formal* journey—an experiment with elements of style which led to the discovery of a layer of "voice" I could call mine, or inhabit, for a period of my life.

First of all I should say that many of these devices might seem on the one hand too obvious to be of use—except to one who doesn't avail herself of them habitually. And, too, that, the taking on, only apparently arbitrary, of stylistic devices—the inhabiting of them until they become the garment of one's spirit life, the method by which one touches the world, the means by which one can be touched oneself, and changed—all of these mysteries are the reason the act of writing holds such powerful and enduring sway over my life. The changes I made in my "technique" are changes that occurred to my life: I became the person I couldn't have otherwise been by these small devices, habits. In other words, the journey is made up of, and created by, technique. The soul-making Keats refers to as the goal of poetry is a web composed of small technical attempts which lead to a new voice—a deeper voice, one at a more morally and historically and spiritually engaged level than the personal voice. A voice one can only build by the *act* of writing, an act which grows dead and automatic if not constantly re-invigorated by strangeness of strategy.

In "San Sepolcro" I tried to slow down the act of *speaking*. I tried all sorts of devices to this end and finally settled on the shortened line, the antiphonal indentation, the singling out of individual words by frequent use of mid-line sentence breaks.

I was delighted in my soul by the slowness of pace I discovered. I started thinking of it (*feeling* it, really) as a kind of solemnity—as when one walks in a cathedral and every sound one makes—footfalls!—seems heightened, significant, held open for inspection, *accountable*. I liked what for me felt like a new nakedness—as if the underpinnings were visible on the surface and no lies could be masked. I have always troubled the area surrounding the "veracity" of an assertion or an image—and so the slowness the indentation thrust upon my habitual way of proceeding thrilled me by its sense of *enforced, solemn, accountability*. Every word seemed suddenly to matter *on its own*—it seemed to resist the kind of easier truthfulness, easier beauty, the sentence could effortlessly (deceitfully?) effect. So: word vs. sentence—fragment brought to the surface. And yet a surface that still had an insistent patterning, order, of its own.

Connected to all this was my (at the time rather terrifying) use of direct address: "In this blue light / I can take you there." Its use flew in the face of all other imagined listeners I had imagined or posited unconsciously up to that point. It forced me down into a far more intimate *voice*—at least tonally intimate—not *personally* intimate.

And this led, I believe, to the use of far more contemporary (vernacular) details (the airplane factory, the assembly line, etc.)—it is the specific admixture—the intermingling without dilution of the dramatic difference—of the spiritual and the physical worlds in this poem that led to the impetus for the writing of the whole book, *Erosion*. The two levels of "going-in" were actually sprung into *life* for me by the sudden appearance of the airplane factory (more than the open-air market which seemed, still, to partake of the aesthetic and historical Italian landscape). The factory—actually glimpsed rounding the hill off Montefalco (so *ugly*, I thought at the time, marring the "view")—the new Italy, if you will—helped me *turn*, in my spirit life, back to Italy and my whole past (family, inheritance, the problematics of memory—historical and personal—the *history*, the wars Europe endured, etc.).

I don't think I could have gotten to the place in my "role of soul-making" where I turned back to Italy and that constellation of aesthetic/historical and personal problems without that airplane factory. I had despaired of ever being able to make the landscape of my *actual* childhood and its art (so utterly literal to me as I played hide-and-seek in the churches of Trastevere as a child) anything other than symbolic or otherwise "unreal" in the context of the America I was living and writing in. The sudden, thrilling, jarring appearance of that airplane factory changed the whole situation. In that sense it actually created a juncture out of which a stage in the journey would unfold.

Our subject matter, the Poem as Journey, or the Journey at the Heart of Poetry, is surely the largest, most extensive that exists in the art. From Homer through Dante and Chaucer, through Shakespeare and Milton, through Leopardi and Goethe, through Zanzotto and Luzi, there is everything to be said and nothing more to say. It is one of those subjects you shadowbox with, since everyone who has ever written who was any good at all is an example to hold up to the light. For every good poem, as we've said, contains a serious journey. Dante, Homer, Chaucer, Shakespeare—what's to say? Eliot, Pound, Akhmatova, Mandelstam, Yeats and Lorca, Milosz and Hikmet: the list might run as long as memory and appreciations permit.

Still, a few more words, perhaps. About Theodore Roethke, an American poet of the generation of Lowell, Berryman, Elizabeth Bishop, and Randall Jarrell. He subsumed the exterior landscape into his interior journey as well, if not better, than anyone in the United States in the second half of this century. His major work is a group of longish long-line meditations on the self, existence, and the landscape entitled "North American Sequence." Six poems that delve into the heart of the American landscape and into the heart of the spiritual self, the long voyage inward through the rocky creekbeds and river gulches, the windy cliffs that contain the dark wave-edge of the soul.

At least I thought that when I first read these remarkable, underappreciated, very American masterpieces. Like Dante's journey, his ends in an image of the rose—in Roethke's case an actual one, though its literary and religious reverberations are unmistakable—a rose in the soul's wind, which tears at reality and the difficult beliefs we sometimes choose to live our lives by.

Roethke, like Hart Crane, has the courage and vision in these poems to go the length of the dead-end road, the road that disappears into the vast expanse of unknowing and incredulity inside us, to come to the end of that road and keep on going; the courage to take the landscape and its significance on its own terms, to take the soul and the soul's self on their own terms and try to come to a workable spiritual balance with them. This is, of course, hard to do, and most writers, like most people, usually avoid it at any cost. Roethke's triumph is that he was fearless in his pursuit of himself and his place in the American literary and spiritual landscape.

As I noted a moment ago, there is just so much one can say in general about a topic as large as ours, and I think I have had my say for the time being. One final comment, though, and a slightly more personal one.

W. B. Yeats, the great Irish poet, wrote once in a verse that when he had said what he had to say, and had begun to enumerate old themes, he had to go back to the starting point: "I must lie down where all the ladders start, / In the foul rag-and-bone shop of the heart." Presumably to start contemplating the real ladder again. This is, of course, the void I was talking about earlier, out of which all journeys begin and to which they all return.

The journey my own poems took, and continue along, may have physically begun at Lake Garda in March, 1959, where I finally found a ladder I had to climb, but the first rung of that journey, out of the heart's void, was surely taken the afternoon a week later when my Volkswagen made a sharp turn on *La Futa* around a cypress tree and I was confronted with the enormity of Brunelleschi's dome on S. Maria del Fiore rising, it seemed, almost out of the road itself in front of me, so near, so huge, the sunlight flashing off its curves and angles. And once we descended, the dome coming into and out of view, ever closer and larger, there was never a turning back.

Improvisations on Donald Justice

I. Jump Hog or Die

Only critics, as Don himself once observed, should be ful-some in their praise. Still, I would like to make a few observa-tions. There was, I felt, always a concentration, always a kind of fierce intensity in his demeanor—a seriousness that spoke to the seriousness of his calling. This was thirty years ago, in the autumn of 1961, my first encounter with Don in the workshop. As far as I know, in such matters—poetry and teaching—such a disposition persists. It was something in him I admired greatly.

The Iowa Writers' Workshop, as everyone must know by now, was run in those days out of Paul Engle's back pocket, and was housed in some leftover Quonset huts: left over from the post–World War II influx of students on the GI Bill. As is usual in such cases, the students went on and the huts remained—married student housing on one side of the Iowa River, art and writing classes on the other. Don and Paul were the only teachers in those days, joined by Mark Strand in my second year when he was brought up from the student ranks. Since Paul was often forced to be on the road looking for dough, Don became, more or less, the poetry workshop. And that was a good thing, at least for me, someone in need of much instruction and direction, someone, literally, just off the boat—a troop ship from Italy. Not all the instruction was found in the workshop, however. A good bit was after hours and interspersed.

Monday afternoons, workshop over, a group would walk from the Quonset hut to the Student Union. To the Ping-Pong room. Don, Mark, Marvin Bell, Bill Brady, Al Lee, Wm Brown, myself, and sometimes others. This was when I first got the notion that Don's fierce intensity was not limited to things ethereal. Did we play vigorous Ping-Pong, or what? Mark was a good player; I was all right, a journeyman; Bill Brady was all right. But Don was very good. I couldn't beat him. Mark may have a couple of times; and Marvin, who was also a good player. But Don was both tough and tenacious, a trait I later saw on the softball field, at the poker table, at the game board (we're talking horse-racing games and war games here), anywhere. For myself, once I discovered poetry, nothing else *really* mattered. I'd tend to drift off if the game at hand wasn't going my way. I lost, in effect, my killer instinct if, in fact, I ever had one. Not Don. *Everything* mattered. It was *all* important. Perhaps not equally, but it all had to be done full bore. It was a quality of participation I envied greatly, but was unable to emulate. But I did play. We all played. But Don *played*. Such intensity. Such an unreturnable serve!

As I say, this concentration was much in evidence in his teaching as well. I shall never forget my first conference with Don to go over my poems. It was, in fact, my first conference with *anyone* about my poems, and I was anxious, to say the least. The subject matter of our conversation—Don's conversation—escapes me now. Some ineptitude I was trying to suggest was a poem. Something, no doubt, about goddesses and the Aegean Sea. But Don, as was his manner, was taking it seriously, very seriously. Certainly more seriously than I, having already seen in a couple of workshop sessions what the level of performance was, a level far above what I was doing. In any case, Don was patiently going over the poem. At the same time, a fly was going over it too. And over us, circling our heads, circling the page, circling Don's face as he kept his concentration ardently on the poem and on what he was saying. I, of course, was mesmerized by the fly as it got closer and closer to Don's face, and, abruptly, as Don inhaled to say something, flew into his mouth. His mouth! Don gulped. Bye fly. He actually swallowed the damn thing, so intent was he on the poem at hand. "Did I swallow that fly?" he asked, astonished. I allowed as to how he had. "Jesus," he said. Amazing! Then he actually went back to the poem. From that moment, he had me in the palm of his hand.

Stories. Many stories. Some repeatable, some not. Nights at Kenney's Tavern. The Famous Pig Roast at Nick Crome's farm where Don organized a high-jumping contest over the pig still on the spit, the coals still glowing. Couples straying impassioned in the burgeoning spring leaves and long grasses of the adjoining fields. Hatchet-throwing competition. Later, knife-throwing contests in Al Lee's apartment, the knives and the distances getting larger and longer. Competition. Much competition. It had a wonderful effect on one's poems. The push to get them written. The desire to get them written right for the proper praise from the proper people.

Don was in the early stages of the *Night Light* poems then. I was in the early stages of learning *The Summer Anniversaries,* almost by heart. I learned what meter was about from his poems. The first successful poem I wrote at Iowa (it took me seven months) was an imitation of the meters and structure in "Landscape with Little Figures." He was a teacher in the best possible ways—he opened you to what was possible and was impeccable in his own work. Surely, as he might say himself, a winning combination.

That was 1961–63. I went away for two years with my MFA degree to the capitals of Europe. When I came back for a second (shorter-lived) go-round in 1965, Mark had gone to New York City and Marvin was teaching. And Don. This was a good time for his poems. He wrote many, especially in syllabics. And since he was writing in syllabics, we were writing in syllabics. The old order was starting to break apart and a new, looser order was looming.

As always in Iowa City, it was a good time to be there. I remember one night I saw him going from town back down to the Quonset huts, to his office, and asked where he was off to. "I've got an idea for a poem," he said. It turned out a few days later to be "The Missing Person." Nelson Algren was in residence that year. Marathon high-stakes poker games. Classes on Stevens and Williams. "Variations for Two Pianos," "The Man Closing Up." I still can't read *Night Light* without an almost unbearable nostalgia. For the things we did, for the poems that were written, for who we were, for our gloriously happy and unhappy selves. There was never a better teacher. There were never better poems to learn from. He is the Thin Man. Such rich refusals!

II. Homage to the Thin Man

The Thin Man

I indulge myself
In rich refusals.
Nothing suffices.

I hone myself to
This edge. Asleep, I
Am a horizon.

I don't know much about Southern poetry as a genre, but there are a couple of Southern poets whose work I have admired and learned from. Perhaps not learned as much as I should have, but have learned a little from, nevertheless. Those two poets are John Crow Ransom and Donald Justice. I have admired things, and admired them greatly, in other poets, especially Robert Penn Warren and James Dickey, both of whom have a narrative power and seduction I find, at times, almost irresistible. But the progenitors to whom I keep coming back, and to whose work my heart continues to lie open, are Ransom and Justice. And of the two, it's Justice I'd like to say a few words about, Ransom having already his place in history, thank you very much, and deservedly so, while Justice seems to me, if not exactly overlooked or neglected (He has won the Pulitzer Prize for his *Selected Poems* and the Bollingen Prize for "lifetime achievement"), certainly a contemporary master whose public ink is nowhere near his poetic achievement.

Poets are like restaurants—as soon as they are successful, they are imitated. Really good poets are like really good restaurants—they are inimitable, though one is continuously nourished there.

We don't say enough about our teachers. Writers are afraid to talk about their teachers, either out of ego, or the anxiety of influence, or both. They are afraid to admit whom they've read, whose writing has changed their lives, as they all wish to have exited the head of Zeus on their own steam. Good luck. We are all a product of who we read and who told us what. All of us, every man-jack and woman-jill.

Justice's poetic production, like Larkin's—the contemporary poet whose career his most resembles, and whose stature he should most share—has been relatively small, four books plus a couple of selected volumes. Still, it's only small compared to, say, Pound or Williams, not to Hopkins or Crane or Bishop, for instance. Moderate production, major results. Like Larkin's, Justice's work is studded with minor masterpieces, several of which (for instance, the villanelle, "Variations for Two Pianos," the sestina, "Here in Katmandu," "The Thin Man" in syllabics, "Sonatina in Yellow," "Counting the Mad") are permanent examples of the form or nonce form. Very few of us can claim to have written a clutch of classics. Justice could, though he probably wouldn't. For Justice and James Merrill are the two unequivocal masters of formal verse in our time. Others are accomplished, indeed, even more wide ranging. But Justice and Merrill are the *maestri*. One has gotten his just due, the other not.

One of the reasons Justice's reputation has not yet kept pace with the excellence of his work, I think, is because he was, for so many years, considered *the* teacher of poetry writing in this country who taught at *the* program of creative writing, the University of Iowa. Those of Justice's generation whose reputations did flourish—Merrill, for example, Merwin, Ginsberg, Creeley, Ashbery—for years had no permanent academic position. Merwin and Merrill still don't, though the others have recently sought academic sanctuary. Also, Justice has a PhD, another impediment to being a "real" poet. Such nonsense. Look at the work instead, the tensile strength and experience of the language, the expansion of the tradition, the invention in formal structures and meters. Teachers. Think of the great painters of past centuries. All teachers with their workshops and apprentices. Are they any less painters of brilliance? I think not. One of the great heroes of the counterculture, Ezra Pound, longed all his life for an academic appointment. Please, no more idle talk about "professor poets." Let's look at the work.

Is it better to be a "little master" than a big failure? Perhaps yes, perhaps no. Some, like the aforementioned Pound, and Hart Crane, are both at the same time. Others in both camps are neither. A golden bird in the hand . . .

What a teacher can supply: clarity of line and clarity of vision, patience for what's good and impatience with what's bad, quality and quantity in the metric tools of the trade and quality and quantity in the history of the discipline, the knowledge that one is always a servant of the language and never more. If the teacher's poems are exemplary themselves, it's a powerful show-and-tell.

Not only are Justice's poems exemplary, his entire enterprise has been. He has been an Alp of integrity to two generations of young poets. His work has not only withstood the mistrals and siroccos of fashion and trendiness, it has also withstood their seductive subtle breezes as well, and has remained true to its constant demand—write clearly, write well. He has written poems, beautiful poems, in all meters and many forms. He has written plays, stories, and essays. So far as I know, he has never written a novel, but I daresay he has contemplated more than one over the years. Distilled, his writing could serve as a hornbook for any aspiring poet. And, as Walter Benjamin said, "An author who teaches writers nothing, teaches no one."

Every poem that Donald Justice ever wrote is a learning experience for the young poet—and the not-so-young poet, too, I might add. There is a problem being either solved, worked on, or worked on and abandoned in each poem that has survived. That these solutions are so liquid and effortless seeming only speaks, of course, to the mastery that went into them. Pick any poem, at random, in the *Selected Poems* or *A Donald Justice Reader* and you will see what I mean— theorems are being worked out, equations are being solved, the abstract is being made palpable, the invisible forces are being brought to light. This is the emotion, these cadences, that endures, as Pound would have it.

He is the contemporary master of the adverb (most notably, perhaps, "perhaps"), both when evident and, especially, when suppressed, though he has said he considers the conjunction the most beautiful part of speech.

Another interesting thing about teachers who are good writers—not only do you get their own take on everything, you also get the people who formed them. And if, as I say, the teacher is an exemplary writer himself, you get these influences condensed and distilled, essences, as it were. Justice's debts to and allegiances with Auden and Stevens have been acknowledged (almost every poet born during the 1920s was influenced by Stevens and Auden). Less well known, but more pervasive in a transparent way, is the light thrown on his work by Rafael Alberti and, especially, Rilke, the early Rilke of *The Book of Pictures* and *New Poems*. The nostalgia, sadness, melancholia and sense of a world lost and a time lost (especially of childhood and adolescence) in both these poets shine like a sunrise, or sunset, over many of Justice's poems, brightening and clarifying, darkening and adumbrating them, outlining their own singularity and substance.

That's about what I wanted to say. Dante put his teacher, Brunetto Latini, in hell, though not because of his teaching. I would put mine, Donald Justice, merely before your eyes, which I hope is not the same place. Reader, read his poems, they *are* addressed to you.

2

Narrative of the Image

A Correspondence with Charles Simic

(At the beginning of spring term, 1994, in my graduate po-
etry writing workshop, I handed out to all the students a copy
of the little statement below. I had manufactured it because I
thought the work of one student—work I liked but that was
somewhat difficult to discuss in the "normal" ways one talks
about such things—wasn't getting the proper attention or en-
couragement it merited. I thought its progression was differ-
ent in concept from more usual practices. I think the class was
somewhat nonplussed by my statement—perhaps rightly—
and I later said so to my friend Charles Simic the next time we
talked on the telephone. He immediately said, "Send it to me.
I'll let you know what I think." His first "Dear Professor W"
letter is what he thought. My first "Commendatore" letter was
my response to him, and we continued on through the spring
until we had insulted each other sufficiently.)

If it is true (and I think it is) that an image is, as Pound put it,
an intellectual and emotional complex in an instant of time,
and if the "logic of metaphor" is, as Crane put it, constructed
on a series of associational meanings and thought-extension,
then the narrative of image and the narrative of metaphor
are different, if not generically then surely perceptively, and
poems employing them will act and react differently. The
narrative (or logic) of metaphor will be more of a time-
release agent, giving the reader a slower, longer contempla-
tion; more time to think about the associations. The poem is
perhaps more susceptible to a flow-through story line *inside*

the poem. The narrative (logic) of image, on the other hand, is more explosive, gives the reader less time to ruminate, opens itself to impressionistic perceptions. The flow, such as it is, is intermittent, interrupted, and tends to exist *outside* the poem, as though a series of things glimpsed quickly, but indelibly, from a fast train. A difference not in kind (as both are defined as "figures of speech") but in degree. But a difference nevertheless, although this is not written down in any book.

Dear Professor W.

Here are some comments (ideas) for your mulling over:

—Image (eye) versus Metaphor (imagination, intellect).
—What kind of Image? With eyes open or with eyes closed?
—Imagism or Surrealism? Please explain.
—Image (in its Imagist version) is the frozen present, its "narrative" doesn't take place in time. Image leads to Vision which is a mystic concept. Vision is close to wordlessness. One uses certain kinds of images to escape or transcend language. Like pointing a finger.
—Metaphor unravels the imaginative (narrative) possibilities of juxtaposed images. If the final goal of Image is Vision, the final goal of Metaphor is Myth which, of course, is a narrative derived from taking the figurative literally.

The function of image is descriptive while the strategy of metaphor is to divest itself of its function of direct description in order to reach the mythic level where its function of discovery is set free. Lots of words ensue from that.

Image is about austerity; metaphor about plenitude . . .

(to be continued)

Commendatore—

It's true the image is less and metaphor is more. As the Master said, for knowledge, add, for wisdom, take away. The Image is Zen, Metaphor is Christian.

If the image, indeed, is descriptive, then the narrative of image *is* traceable, though traceable as footprints are in a rapidly warming snow, distinct but always on the edge of disappearance. Thus, one *could*, I suppose, make the case for an imagistic story line inside the poem, but one always on the verge of vanishing once it had been discovered. Still, the story line outside the poem remains, I think, the stronger one imagistically.

As St. John of the Cross said, to know your road, you must close your eyes and walk in the dark. I would say the same thing about the image. The true image rises out of the darkness—sometimes it stays there and only its luminous outline is traceable; sometimes it is out in the open, and only its luminous outline is traceable, a pentimento against the seen world. The true image belongs to neither Imagism nor Surrealism. It belongs to the Emptiness. Which is to say its power is otherworldly and ultimately apophatic, a luminous outline above the tongue. (The false image, of course, is all too readily apparent and glad-handing.) All of this merely to agree with your assertion that the progression is image to vision to wordlessness. But to disagree that there is a separation, at the ultimate level, imagistically between Surrealism and Imagism. That distinction exists only in time, not in space, or in that third dimension, outside these two, the image rises from.

Since the narrative of the image doesn't take place in time, as you say, then it seems even more likely that any such narrative will take place outside the temporal borders of the poem itself, and will exist more as a continuous and continuing series of overlays which eventually form the story line by accretion. The inner eye, palimpsesting, covering and uncovering simultaneously.

If myth is the ultimate goal of metaphor, iconolatry is the final resting place of the image.

In all this, metaphor is the old, image the new. Metaphor is memory, the image is prescience . . .

Gnostics are gnarled and gnomic, gnashing their teeth, gnathically gnawing the gnarring gnocchi of truth, which is gnat-like and gneissic. Is their gnomon a gnu? No.

Yours in hypgnosis—

March 3, 1994

Dear Professor W.

What is this "true image" stuff? Have you been hearing voices from those fundamentalist churches in your neighborhood? More likely you've been cracking open stale Zen fortune cookies from your California days?

You speak of metaphysical and transcendental unity between Imagist and Surrealist images, and I say, very nice, but you got to show me. Here in the Calvinist North we don't go for that kind of ecstatic mumbo jumbo just because it sounds good. Consider the following:

A crescent moon in the sky—

This is what Ezra called phanopoeia, your primary image and the one, by the way, easiest to translate.

But, and this is a big BUT, if like the riddle-maker, I detect an unexpected resemblance up there and blurt out:

Father's scythe is lying across Mother's Sunday skirt!

It seems to me that here we have something different. Or as Meister Eckhart said long ago: "An image takes its being immediately and solely from that of which it is an image of." So, Chief . . .

In image 1, one wishes to convey what is already there. An image like that keeps the demon of analogy at bay. Its purpose is transparency, homage to clear sight.

In image 2, I have redescribed the world. I have conveyed not what it looks like, but what it feels like! I've let the demon, as it were, to play with my marbles. (And, as you well know, he's capable of even wilder stunts.)

Ergo, you say the two images meet in EMPTINESS. How? I don't understand how you reconcile the two? I'm wondering whether such reconciliation is really a betrayal of their lovely distinctness—like saying the eye and ear are really the same organ? I say, come out of the closet all you secret Neoplatonists! Tell us how you see Sharon Stone, Holly Hunter, and Faye Dunaway as one ideal woman! The ass and legs from the first, the tits from the second, and the eyes and hair from the third, and there you have it! Every philosopher's dream date!

In the meantime, I await your clarifications, your further gnostic unscramblings and hosannas with the impatience of a peep-show customer. I even got my tambourine ready!

Cheers,

Chaz

Commendatore—

Okay, okay, I see how this is going to go—you get to be Larkin, I have to be grumpy old Yeats, you get to be Pound, I have to be solemn old Rilke, you get to be Cornell, I have to be morbid old Rothko, you get to be Robin Williams, I have to be Rodney Dangerfield. So be it.

Look, here's a little equation without an equals sign:

Invention—inspiration/the present/the image/words written on ice . . .
Discovery—memory/the past/metaphor/language (the whole pool of the history of . . .)

Let's try the translations:

1) La mezzaluna in cielo . . .
2) La falce del padre (di papà) sta sdriata sulla (per la) gonna domenicale della madre (di mamma)!

This is tricky because it really doesn't work—there are, of course, other languages, there are other translations. Still, you can say that the first is easier to see and the second is easier to imagine. Neither, however, takes the third step—art is the image of an image of an image. The third step, the third image, is the narrative of metaphor. The image (the first image) just starts the story. Thus, you haven't "redescribed the world," you've merely redescribed the image. You'd have to redescribe the rediscription to move on to changing the world.

The narrative of the image is a sprinter, the narrative of metaphor a long-distance runner—the beauty of adagio and the beauty of sostenuto.

It is harder to see yourself at one side of the mirror than directly in front of it. Yet you're there as unmistakably, and the mirror knows it even if it can't see you. And you know it too.

The word "transcendental" never escaped my lips. Neither did "metaphysical." Though they could have (unnatural questions, supernatural elements) had I not been wary. There are some things you can't hear unless you're listening for them. Still, they are, those two, in my vocabulary.

These are the Aphorisms of the Dead:

1. Lie low and keep your own counsel.
2. Never bite with your tongue out.
3. In the Kingdom of the Deaf, nobody hears a thing.
4. The language from one life is untranslatable in the next.
5. Out of the dark into the dark . . .
6. Time never stops, it only stands still.
7. Out of the pigshit into the pigshit . . .
8. No matter how much the snow falls, we never get white.
9. An apple for inference, an orange for pride.
10. God's light is all powerful, but it can't find us.

In spite of what M. Eckhart says, an image has no *being*. It is, as I say, as all art becomes, the image of an image of an image. So it doesn't have being until the third step, when it has become a part of the narrative of metaphor, and metaphor *does* have being. That's why the narrative of image is outside the poem and the picture, and the narrative of metaphor is inside both.

Have I said that the narrative of image is figure skating—double axels and Suchows and spin leaps and death spirals? And the narrative of metaphor is deep sea fishing . . . It's odd, I think. When Pound moved from Imagisme to Vorticism, he said it was because Amy Lowell had co-opted his Imagism movement (made it into Amygism). I also think there was a deeper reason—he knew he was on the surface and wanted to dive under, to make the succession of image the succession of metaphor, from the momentary dazzle of flying fish down to the deep pull of the giant marlin, as it were. As he said, he didn't want something "stationary." It was about that time he began the actual writing of the *Cantos,* for instance. The undertow of the narrative of image is light and lightning; that of metaphor is darkness and blood.

We've wandered—which is to say, I've wandered. The narrative of image is the mouth of the cave. The narrative of metaphor is the cave. It always seems to be a question of outside and inside. Both are seductive and have their own beatitudes. Image is the crucifixion, metaphor is the ascension. This can go on and on. Well, not really. There are endings to things. And they are metaphors, not images. Beginnings are images.

Listen, just because the bear's mouth is open doesn't mean he's going to eat you. Maybe he's getting ready to sing. Have faith. Breathe deeply.

Ah, la Donna, the Lady Ideal, Ideale, Na Audiart, as Bertran de Born had her, Lady Maent, he with his own head in his hand, lighting his way along the dike of the 8th Bolgia—to put them together like that, to make the most beautiful woman in Provence, a tit here, an eye for this and an ear for that, sweet cheeks. Well, sure, dream on. There is no reconciliation, none at all. That's why they meet in the generating emptiness of the fantasy of imagination. Where else? *Sacrum, sacrum, inluminatio coitu,* as Pound had it in one of the Cantos (36): "The rite, the rite, illumination in coition." If not there, where? Uncloset me here. Father's scythe may be lying across Mother's Sunday skirt, but his whetstone is back on the moon's edge, and that's still Saturday night. Play a song for me . . .

Here's one, the first stanza to *Dead Pale Penis Person Blues* . . .

> Woke up this morning,
>> my dick was white and lean,
> Woke up this morning,
>> my dick was white and lean,
> Well, you know, pretty mama,
>> you know what that must mean.

Give me a second stanza, Exquisite Corpse. *Ti saluto, Commendatore, e ti auguro una buona Primavera domani—*

March 26, 1994

Dear Professor W.

Hegel was a breeze. I never even broke sweat following the most intricate scholastic arguments of Duns Scotus and Aquinas. That was before I met up with Professor W. and his "Third Step." Now I'm a "mezzaluna in cielo." I don't trust myself to tell the difference between my ass and my elbow. I ask myself, is this how he talks to his wife, the photographer! And how does she reply?

"The third step, the third image, is the narrative of metaphor," says he, and I think, that sounds like a pronouncement of some storefront Maharashi back in the 1960s. He expects to chant "OM" in reply. The problem for me, dear Lama, is that I don't know what you mean by "narrative of metaphor?" Are you talking about myth? Are you saying that a poem is an extension of a single metaphor like myth? And what about "narrative of images"? Is it like the movies?

Perhaps the beginning of my confusion lies with you placing "the present/the image" under INVENTION in your "little equation." How can the present be invented? What happened to consciousness and clear sight? Didn't they teach you anything in that flea-ridden lamaserai?

"It is the peculiarity of the true poet that his word creates actuality, calls forth and unveils something real," said one

Anagarika Govinda. Where do we, mortal folk, locate that in your jewel-studded EQUATION, O Master? Once you tell us, "the Aphorisms of the Dead" should be a snap. The same goes for "light" and "lightning" and the Wagnerian "darkness" and "blood." (I kind of fancy "Image is the crucifixion, metaphor is the ascension," but we need to know how we got there, and we haven't done that yet.)

The temptation in any such discussion, as the one we are having, is to dangle a shiny rhetorical object before the eyes of your listener, make him or her fall under a spell and follow you wherever you want to. You and your reader end up living inside your metaphors like apes in a forest. It's fun, of course! There's a lot of chest-pounding and yelling at the top of one's voice, but that's all. So, let's see if this brings us all down from the trees?

I made a tiny hole in the wall with a long nail so that I could watch them screw. Image is what I saw; metaphor is when my tongue caught fire. If it's the image I wish to employ it is because I want you to stand in my shoes and make you see what I saw. Isn't that the purpose of all art, the hope that by and by you too will become I? Anyway, where you see continuity between image and metaphor, I see a gap. Yes, one sets off the other, but only to lose something and gain something else in the process. What is left behind in the image when one leaps on the first metaphor that comes along? Plenty, I think. I would like to comprehend this stage of the game before I venture into a beautific synthesis of the two, in which I also secretly believe, but am in no rush to get to yet.

And now, in my never-ending pursuit of the elusive spark of Illumination, I'm going to the town dump with my dog, Samson.

Cheers,

Chaz

Commendatore—

The simile, caro Commendatore, the *right* simile, is the key to the kingdom. As such, like all sacred things, it should be used sparingly and wisely and only when justified, if at all, and perhaps not even then. It should never be abused.

The equation is always darkness and light, of course, but our balance is wrong. We go from light to darkness; therefore the equation is light = darkness, not the other way round. Why is it we do not see this?

Re: inside and outside (narrative of metaphor, narrative of image) that we began this with: outside tends to drift away, it is less anchored, it tends toward width; inside tends toward depth, containment, and stability. Bachelard says, "*This side* and *beyond* are faint repetitions of the dialectics of inside and outside: everything takes form, even infinity." Now that's a Zen zone I could cotton to. It also, from my point of view, reinforces my preference for a narrative of metaphor over that of image. The implied *vastness* (as Bachelard terms it) of the outside—since the narrative of image generally has no denouement to its sequencing—becomes more of the surround than that which is surrounded, and thus more incapable of clarification and definition. Even if the infinite has form, it is more mythic than moral, i.e., more inhuman than human. For some, I suppose, this is a good thing. Here, there, this side, that side, inside, outside, trope upon trope . . . Perhaps, in the ultimate sequence and consequence, there *is* no denouement. In that case, the narrative of image is the language they speak there. But, for the moment, we are here, and words fill our earthly mouths . . .

To repeat: the narrative of image has no closure. It is never finished, only abandoned. (As Valery said, incorrectly, of the poem.)

There is a photograph—a rather famous photograph, actually, which you probably know well—of the French artist Yves Klein jumping out of a high window to the street. The picture catches him in mid-jump, coat-and-tied, stretched out, his foot just clearing the stone wall behind him, a man on a bicycle disappearing down the street, nothing between him and the stone pavement but air. Now, I ask you, is this photograph, is the story of this "image," the narrative of image or the narrative of metaphor? As it turns out, the whole "happening" or "conceptual piece" was a total metaphor, as the photograph is a trick. There was a net set to catch Klein, which did so in the original jump. The photograph of the jump was then cut just above the net, and another bottom (which included the bicyclist not in the original) was collaged onto the jumping figure, the whole rephotographed and, *voilà*, we have Yves declining into the void, sans net, giving us a false narrative of image when, in fact, the whole story was a metaphor. Ah, photography, as no art is . . . Still, it's a great picture, and art is always subjunctive, subjective, secretive, and siderial. Yves! The void is just under our bodies, just under the net.

(Actually, there were two versions of the photograph, one with the bicyclist and one without, both collages. *Still,* if one did *not* know they were both—or either—collages, a real case could be made for the one *without* the bicyclist being read as a narrative of image, as it presupposes no closure or further story, and the one with the velocipede and rider as a narrative of metaphor, if only because the added element, human element, becomes a reactive agent. But . . .).

Now, what you saw through that hole in the wall was, politically correctly, image on top of metaphor. On top, but metaphor was still inside and image outside, no matter her position. A gap, yes, but it opens and closes. How far apart they are, how inseparable.

Ah, the lamaserai . . . The clear sound of the water drops, the slow urge of the stream as it made its way effortlessly under the banyan trees and out of sight. We each saw it only one time. Tell me, Commendatore, if you know, are water drops an image in their ruin, and in their gathered stream a metaphor? How can we tell the droplet from the stream? It all appeared so apparent back then, the lamaserai so one and so individual at once, and we, too, the echo of one thing and the echo of all things at the same time. Ah, those were the days!

Up in the trees. Of course, that's where the poem always takes us—the "shiny rhetorical object" before our eyes *is* the poem. Where else do we live but in our own constructions? (As they used to tell us back in the lamaserai—"Look lovingly on some object. Do not go on to another object. Here, in the middle of this object—*the blessing.*" They also used to say—"Objects and desires exist in me as in others. So accepting, let them be *translated.*" That's what you said too.) What other architecture for apes like us? And of course the present is invented. One's whole existence is invented as one receives and transforms it. Then it goes through and around us into the past, which always stays as it is—as does the future. Only that which we can get our image-and-metaphor-making fingers on can be invented. You can *reinvent* the other two, but that's a different narrative, isn't it?

Listen, I don't *know* what the narrative of image and the narrative of metaphor are, either. But, then, I don't know what they're *not,* either. That's why we're doing this. Still, there *are* answers. Here's one:

1. Nothingness is not nothing . . .

Here's another:

2. All things that are the same are different . . .

So, for the time being, I'm waiting here with my cat, Delilah, hoping not to catch the wrong train, waiting for your reply—

April 20, 1994

Dear Professor W.

Okay, let me attempt a definition of the narrative of the image and see if you agree.

I see a man jumping out of a window, I gasp, my eyes open wide, the sight hits me like a bolt of lightning! As I become conscious of what I'm seeing and of myself noticing the details and explaining to myself the circumstances and the outcome of the fall, the narrative of the image truly starts. The image properly is not in time; the narrative is the unraveling in time of its ramifications and its plot.

Now here's the trick. The image (and this applies to the visual aspect of the metaphor too) must be powerful. You need the shock of consciousness to get the narrative going. Some images can write epics, others have barely enough in them for a haiku. An ideal image, like the sun, would be an almost endless generator of imaginative energy.

Narrative is a term, you'll agree Professor, that unfortunately does not convey the full range of activity that results from our encounter with an image or a metaphor. What makes things complex and confusing is that we experience images with our intellect as well as with our emotions and our senses. "No ideas but in things," said the famous baby doctor from New Jersey, and that applies here too. The narrative of the image will differ depending on what part of ourselves does the unraveling. If the intellect starts fucking with it, for instance, the outcome is a symbol. If our emotions and imagination are involved, a metaphor will be the result. There is also the additional possibility, as the Surrealists suspected, that we have nothing to do with the narrative. Words tell each other stories and we just sign the checks.

Whatever the case may be, I regard the image as the cause of all narratives. I also believe that the narrative in time must never betray its original moment. The goal of each narrative must be to recover the freshness of the first impact of the image. I'm thinking of the initial image as a kind of Eden and the narrative as the exile. This ought to appeal to your Old Testament, Kingsport, Tennessee, revival meeting ethos. My own authority in such cases is, as always, my insomnia. For what else is insomnia, but the narrative of the image?

Does this make sense? I hope so. I'm in a hurry to get to more important matters, Professor. What about the influence of a bottle of noble vintage on the narrative of the image? Can diet soda make the demon of analogy happy? Don't you think that reading most contemporary poets one would have to conclude that they have never been to the movies? I know for a fact that they have never heard a country fiddle or a banjo playing!

The only narrative of the image that does it justice is music.

Yours,

C. S.

Commendatore—

You spoke, in your next-to-last letter, as though you thought poems have consequences in the world. Do you? I don't. I think of them as aesthetic possibilities, objects of beauty and contemplation, not rallying points or calls for action. Unless, of course, within their own spheres of influence, which is, naturally, themselves and their ancestors and progeny.

I often think, or today I think, of the narrative of image as a kind of asphalt-making paving machine that lays the surface down as it drives along: it creates its own surface as it slides across the skeleton of the poem. The narrative of metaphor, on the other hand, seems like a river that works its way under ground, creating its own space, enlarging that space as it deepens and cuts. Whole hidden architectures and subterranean structures start to develop. The logic of image seems to me more straightforward and easily observed, closer to "narrative" in the common, observable sense. It's more shiny and readily seen. Metaphor takes the darker side. It is the narrative of the dead. (It's not lost on me that one of my figures [for image] is man-made and the other [for metaphor] is natural.)

In a poem composed either in the narrative of image or in the narrative of metaphor, we are always one line short. Why is this?

Whether the poem is composed by narrative of image or narrative of metaphor, form must flow through the poem as wind flows through the air . . .

Second verse to *Dead Pale Penis Person Blues:*

> I'm History's fool,
>> you know I'm riptide bound,
> Well, I'm History's fool,
>> you know I'm riptide bound,
> So look for me, pretty mama,
>> look for me out and down.

Sleep, our two-dimensional sidekick, without foreground or background, has no memory: flat dreamlight, light like aluminum foil, depthless . . . Its images two-dimensional, the narrative of them the same, no memory, one-sided, ungathered. Dreaming is image, waking is metaphor. O butterfly, O nightingale . . .

A narrative of the image is hydroponic—it exists and sustains itself on its own surface, or on that which provides its own surface. Or else it is Pothotic and exists on air and desire . . .

Here's a third, and last, verse:

> Gone before my time,
>> I'm all hogged down and tied,
> Gone before my time,
>> I'm all hogged down and tied,
> So shamed and lorn, pretty mama,
>> I like to up and died.

Your last letter to hand, and it is a well-considered and apt one, indeed. Do some images grow up to be metaphors and some not (Mamas, don't let your Images grow up to be Metaphors . . .)? I am partial to your thinking of the original image as Eden and the narrative as the exile. And since the narrative is both, in this case, that of image and metaphor, who could ask for more? Chuck Heston hot-footing it down from the mountain, one stone book in either hand, getting ready to move on? There's an old country song, gospel song, "Memories of the Bush on Fire" that should fit in somewhere with your last sentence. Or with the Surrealists—we may just sign the checks, but we also, perhaps, just check the signs.

So, caro Commendatore, I will close out for good now. This was, possibly, all along an atom that did not need splitting, but's it's been an interesting little bang, and music, as they say, to my ears. Here's looking at you, C. I'm much appreciative of the Carter Family stamp on your last envelope, a sign I've checked, a check I've signed.

May 16, 1994

Dear Professor W.

Your last epistle has a certain triumphant air about it. As far as you are concerned, we've caught the black cat of poetry in the dark by its tail. You want to put a pencil behind your ear, and so do I, believe me, but the nagging sense of unfinished business won't let me rest.

I don't think, for instance, that we have done justice to an important aspect of image and metaphor, an aspect that still worries everyone who sits down to write a poem:

—Where do these images and metaphors come from, Professor?
—Why are some caught in the eye and remembered while others are obviously not?
—How come there are moments when one has the eye for the similar and the significant, when for the rest of our days, poets like everyone else stare at the world in incomprehension?
—What role does memory play?
—And what about archetypes?
—If the image concerns sight and the metaphor imagination, for what lofty and base reasons do we go back and forth between literal and figurative?

Poetry is an utterance that no paraphrase can exhaust because poetry is not about ideas but about the music of chance. Poetry proclaims that there's something more real than ideas, something that remains, as it were, always stubbornly unformulated, but which we as readers of poetry have no trouble experiencing and savoring in poems we love. For me, images and metaphors, what we see and what we imagine, their perpetual undermining of each other, their paradox, their ambiguity, their slyness, their mindboggling wisdom and comedy gets at the core of our existence because our existence, too, cannot be paraphrased.

A very drunk professor of philosophy once asked me angrily: What do you poets really want?

I was stumped at the time, told him we want to destroy all the fixed formulas, baked and rebaked little turds of ideas, as Céline would say, but today I would pause to order another round of drinks and say the following:

The secret desire of poetry is to seduce. It uses images and metaphors to lure, entrap, and enslave the unsuspecting. The ancients knew the dangers. If it were only "virgin youths" the poets were putting under a spell, it would be bad enough already, but their outrage aims even higher. They want to seduce gods and devils by way of something they don't even understand themselves. Admit, Professor, you often secretly hoped that one of your dazzling images and metaphors would summon the Lord! That you would feel the breath of his astonishment and of his envy on your smirking face! You probably did, since you're a true poet washed in the blood of the lamb. Otherwise, what would this endeavor be really worth? The ambition of each image and metaphor is to redescribe the world, or, more accurately, to blaspheme. Stevens knew that and Dickinson suspected it. That's why they kept a low profile. The truth of poetry is a scandal. A thousand naked fornicating couples with their moans and contortions are nothing compared to a good metaphor.

I'm blowing the siren! Ringing the church bells! Good people of Virginia, start gathering kindling for the stake! Professor Wright is bringing his own matches!

Yrs,

Chaz

Postscript

Since it was my ball originally, I suppose I want the last at-bat, even if I only look at three pitches. I certainly intended nothing "triumphant" about my last letter—I admitted in my first statement to not really knowing the difference between the two types of "narrative" (but intuiting that, somehow, there *was* a difference in how the two types were *put together,* if not perceived) and confessing at the end I still didn't *know* the difference (this is not DNA, of course, this is not a mathematical theorem we are talking about. Hence no "solution"). So, no triumph there. Still, it was fun, and often enlightening, to worry the "problem" around a bit.

We have not done justice to the examples the Commendatore has raised in his last letter. But, then, we weren't supposed to. He ends the argument/discussion as all good arguments/discussions should end—with an opening, not a closing. I would only add a couple of observations to match:

—Poetry is at least as important for what is not said as for what is.
—The secret of poetry is silence, the unheard echoes of utterances that wash through us with their solitary innuendos.
—As the good Commendatore so acutely observes, the ultimate ambition of every good poem is blasphemy, or, surely, a blasphemy. And, I would add, its attendant, speechless undertow, against which image and metaphor act as our gondola and oar, pushing against the unforgiving tide.

3

Bytes and Pieces

—Timing is essence.

—*True* description *is* enactment. I.e., when what is being described is part of the process, it is not static.

—"After the classicism of the early abstractionists, and the romanticism of 'abstract expressionism,' what we need is a Mannerism, a Baroque-abstract." (Octavio Paz in "Language and Abstraction," *Alternating Currents*.) Is the same true in poetry?

—Art is *after* the fact. The real is imaginary (imagined), what we have envisioned before the act—representation, reconstruction, reconstitution, are what we are left with as document.

—Narrative does not dictate the image; the image dictates the narrative.

—One of the differences between poetry and prose is that— good or bad—lines are final. Sentences are never final, but ceaselessly rearrangeable.

—"The impressionist painters, Monet, Sisley especially, had delicate, vibrating sensations; as a result their canvases are all alike. The word 'impressionism' perfectly characterizes their intentions for they register fleeting impressions . . . A rapid rendering of a landscape represents only one moment of its

January 1988–December 1990.

appearance. I prefer, by insisting upon its essentials, to discover its more enduring character and content, even at the risk of sacrificing some of its pleasing qualities ... Underneath this succession of moments which constitute the superficial existence of things animate and inanimate and which is continually obscuring and transforming them, it is yet possible to search for a truer, more essential character which the artist will seize so that he may give to reality a more lasting interpretation . . ."

—Matisse, *Notes of a Painter* (1908)

—"Before I began studying Zen, I saw mountains as mountains, rivers as rivers. When I learned some Zen, mountains ceased to be mountains, rivers ceased to be rivers. But now, when I have understood Zen, I am in accord with myself and again I see mountains as mountains, rivers as rivers."

—Saisho, as quoted in Milosz, *Unattainable Earth*

—"Every one of us, leaving this life, preserves from the past, from memories, from quotations by which he lived, no more than a few words that he salvages from a receding memory."

—Milosz, *Unattainable Earth*

—You have to advance the medium. Or expand it. Merely to repeat what has been attempted, however marvelously, is nice, but not enough. To become known, you must do it differently; differently with a deeper disregard.

—"Perhaps the best label for him as a painter would be Religious Realist. A realist because he attached supreme importance to the incessant study of nature and never composed pictures 'out his head'; religious because he regarded nature as the sacramental visible sign of a spiritual grace which it was his aim as a painter to reveal to others."

—Auden on Van Gogh

—If you have a story to tell, tell it; if you have a song to sing, sing it. But don't mistake narrative for lyric, don't mistake prose for poetry.

—The Structural Imperative (demiurge of the Formal Imperative) is the one oblation which cannot be substituted for. It must be effected in each poem, and in each poem in a new way. It cannot be obviated.

—My favorite Renaissance painter—in Italy, at least—is Ignoto, especially the one from Ferrara.

—After the New Narrative—or instead of it—is the New Anecdote: for those who have a story to tell, but don't know how to tell it, or for those who have no story to tell, but insist on telling it anyway. Already its practitioners are sharpening their shovels. Already the sound of thrust and squish is being heard throughout the land.

—Style is the ability to see through things—great style is vision.

—Cézanne became a great painter when he deserted forms and discovered structure—when he stopped painting figures from his imagination and discovered his motif, the landscape. He needed to abandon forms to find Form.

—It's all right to be trendy and fashionable (i.e., today, political concerns or language demolition), but someone has to speak up for the quiddity of the whatnot.

—One of the purposes (one of several) of writing the two-step line I have used on and off since 1978, the low-rider, whatever you want to call it, was to be able to keep the line from breaking under its own weight. In other words, my line began to get longer and more "conversational" as I tried to push it as far toward prose as I thought I could and still maintain it as a verse line. So I began to break the line, in order to keep it whole. It is always one line, not two, and broken in a particular place to keep the integrity of the single line musically. Others who have used the broken line (Pound, Williams, Olson, O'Hara—Justice, even, a few times—and others) used it, for the most part, as two lines (in Williams's case, three lines), as separate entities. Mine is almost always one line, and sounds like one line. To my ear, anyhow.

—"One can speak verbal 'music' so long as one remembers that the sound of words is inseparable from their meaning. The notes in music do not denote anything."

—Auden

—I write from the point of view of a monk in his cell. Sometimes I look at the stones, sometimes I look out the window.

—I have no public, or social, aspirations in my work. All my aspirations are private, a locating and defining out of my own life. I wouldn't presume to speak for anyone else.

—In the Scylla (Language Poetry) and Charybdis (New Formalism) of current poetries, there is great camouflage at work. The Language Poets preach the isolation of language and text to cover up the inherent lack of formal properties in their venture, and the New Formalists preach traditional formal vessels to cover up their lack of interest and skill in language power—they hope the forms will give their language the movement, rhythm, beauty, and meaning they themselves are incapable of bringing to it. Their elders knew better— Zukofsky was a formalist of immense vision, as was Frost and Crane. Only free verse makes one work seriously in both areas as it makes its way between these two forces. Or, to change the metaphor, free verse is not, as Frost would have it, like playing tennis without a net, but is the high wire act without the net. It is a kind of Negative Capability. Form is everything along the line of language.

—A deconstructionist critic writing about Language Poetry is like a dog eating its own vomit.

—". . . to award someone a prize is no different from pissing on him. And to receive a prize is no different from allowing oneself to be pissed on, because one is being paid for it." Prizes "do nothing to enhance one's standing, as I had believed before I received my first prize, but actually lower it, in the most embarrassing fashion."

—Thomas Bernhard

—The New Formalists have a problem. They think, for the most part, that the poem fits the form. The Old Formalists knew better—they knew the form had to fit the poem. Big difference.

—I would like my poems to be like visionary frescoes on the walls of some out-of-the-way monastery.

—Add above: I worked in the back room of the monastery. My view was circumscribed, but intense.

—The Map of Poetry goes something like this. There's a long, flat plain made up of good writing, clarity, and emotional insight. Beyond that rises the Great Wall of Language. Beyond that lies the Void. No other configurations.

—*What We Want*

A line that is supple and sure,
A style that is prescient and pure.
As Stein said to Hemingway,
Damn it all, anyway,
Remarks are not Literature.

—"What a mess! I believe in images as vehicles of transcendence, but I don't believe in God."

—Charles Simic

—Add the New Formalists: In their silly recall to nostalgia, they have become the Mr. Goodwrench of contemporary poetry. While, on the other hand, the Language poets continue to be the Joe Isuzu of same.

—My ultimate strength is my contemporary weakness—my subject (language, landscape, and the idea of God) is not of much interest now. But it will be again. How all three configure one's own face is important and must be addressed. Unstable as dust, our lives will find us out.

—The past is a stained glass window. We see it through the door of our monk's cell, so brilliant, so out of reach on the church wall. Behind it, in the dark, when the light comes through at the proper angles, the colors are unimaginably luminous, the scenes of our various selves unspeakably clear, evocative and unbroken.

—One does get tired of the incessant bleating about "form" from the self-proclaimed New Formalists. To repeat: all questions about the putting together of poems are questions about formal values, questions of form. To think "form" concerns only received metrical patterns (i.e., rhyme and iambic meters—or trochaic or anapestic, etc.) is like saying a river isn't composed of water because it has no salt in it; only the oceans are water.

—Good free verse is free in the way that good abstract art is abstract. Which is to say, not very. Who are more formal painters than Mark Rothko and Franz Kline? Not many. Who are more formal poets than Charles Olson and Louis Zukofsky? Not many. Form, of course, always being an application of theoretical values. Never less, never other. Keats's iambic odes, Zukofsky's 5×5s—it's all formal manipulation. Yeats and Pound, Crane and Eliot, Wilbur and Creeley, Justice and Merwin.

—Ambition for one's work and ambition in one's work is both laudatory and necessary. When it devolves to one's person, however, it becomes like the material in a fable that, mixed with water or some other ordinary substance, suddenly becomes poisonous.

—Opinions are easy; convictions are harder to come by. Personal style, for instance, is different from poetic style. The former has been characterized as a form of grace under pressure. The latter, on the other hand, might better be said to be a form of pressure under grace.

—The past is the one mirror that never releases its images. Layer and overlay, year after year, wherever you look, however you look, whenever you look, it's always your own face you see there. All those years, and it's still your own face.

—"In modern western art an object's form is its physical certitude, and though it might change over time—through deterioration or the artist's intent—its form is conceived as the sum of its absolute physical properties. We in the west generally define form in the visual arts in opposition to chaos and change; it is complete and static, the end product of many artistic decisions.

"By contrast, form in Japanese sculpture is conceived to be generated by change or flux itself. Indeed, the concept of completion is antithetical to much contemporary Japanese art: form is an event within an ongoing process that never truly ends. This concept is not new in Japanese culture and can be found at its very heart. Near the city of Ise in south-central Japan is Shinto's most important national sanctuary, the Great Shrine. There, in the midst of a densely wooded and rugged terrain, a wooden wall encloses an acre or two of stark, perfectly flat land; within that sanctified place, a second wooden barrier ritually demarcates a second *kami* zone; at its center stands a wooden tabernacle or ark that for 2,000 years has contained Shinto's most sacred objects: the mirror and the polished jewels that, according to the first imperial chronicles, were used to coax the sun goddess Amaterasu out of hiding, thereby restoring light to the world and ultimately enabling the creation of her descendants, the Japanese race and its imperial clan.

"The Great Shrine is an ancient and enduring place, but every twenty years since the 7th century the shrine has been completely dismantled and rebuilt—identical in every detail— with new wood. This rebuilding is, of course, as much a ritual of renewal and rebirth as it is a maintenance activity, but it is also a manifestation of the Japanese notion of physical form as a provisional arrangement of parts in time and space. The sacred precinct of Ise remains a fixed and constant place; as a physical object the shrine has been discarded again and again for the past 1300 years. To western perception, the rebuilding of the shrine causes another shrine to exist, but to the Japanese it is the same shrine in the same place, having the same function, suffused with the same holiness, containing the same *kami*."

—Howard N. Fox, *A Primal Spirit*

—The two best lyricists of the 1960s were Bob Dylan and James Tate.

—If a photograph is a message without a code, as Barthes says, then my poems are codes without a message.

—"Architecture is, self-evidently, landscape. But so, in degrees of increasing psychological internalization, are paintings, statues, verbal representations of the human and the natural manner of things and, most subtly, those musical dispositions of time and of space which, in ways we fully experience even if we cannot as yet rationalize them, change the felt pulse of our daily lives."

—George Steiner, *Real Presences*

—The difference between nothing and not-nothing is a line drawn on the air. One must try to draw this line.

—"Nothing can be left out, but you have to bury the irrelevant *in* the picture, somehow."

—Frank Auerbach

—Subject matter is like an almond in a Hershey bar—nice but not necessary.

—"When the ten thousand things have been seen in their unity, we return to the beginning and remain where we have always been."

—T'Sen Shen

—"It is imitation that has progressed into individuality; it is a psychological symptom akin to tone of voice and personality; it is a skill, an extension of character, an attitude toward the world, an enigma."

—Guy Davenport on "Style"

—Poetry is language that sounds better and means more . . .

Addendum/1993

—The heart of nature is nature, the heart of landscape is God. Which is to say, the heart of nature is disease (and disease), and the heart of landscape is design (*dasein*).

—Landscape is something you determine and dominate; nature is something that determines and dominates you.

—Nature is inherently sentimental, landscape is not.

—As in Francis Bacon's self-portraits, the more distorted the image becomes, the more figurative it becomes. So in poetry the more abstract the poem becomes, the more formal it gets in execution.

—Landscape is a "distancing" factor (description of same, identification of self in same) as regards the "self," the "I" in poetry. Nature, on the other hand, is quicksand.

—"The truer a work of art is, the more it has a style. Which is strange, because style is not truth of appearances, and yet the heads which I find most like those of people one sees in the street are the least realistic heads, the heads of Egyptian, Chinese, or archaic Greek sculpture. For me, the greatest inventiveness leads to the greatest likeness."

—Alberto Giacometti

4

The Art of Poetry XLI

Charles Wright
(with J. D. McClatchy)

[From his dust-jacket photographs, you might expect Charles Wright to be a dour man. In person, though, he gives a quite different impression—trim, elegant even in blue jeans, generous, with a Southerner's soft-spoken courtliness. Born in Pickwick Dam, Tennessee, in 1935, he grew up in the South and went to college there. And a few years ago, after a long spell of teaching at the University of California at Irvine, he returned to the South, as poet-in-residence at the University of Virginia.

Wright's work stands out among his generation of poets for the austere luxuriance of its textures, its mingling of domestic subjects and foreign methods, and its bold and unpretentious ambition. During the past two decades he has written eight books of poems: *The Grave of the Right Hand* (1970), *Hard Freight* (1973), *Bloodlines* (1975), *China Trace* (1977), *The Southern Cross* (1981), *Country Music: Selected Early Poems* (1983; winner of that year's National Book Award in Poetry), *The Other Side of the River* (1984), and *Zone Journals* (1988). He has also translated two volumes of poetry, by Eugenio Montale and Dino Campana, and when I visited him he was putting together a collection of prose writings.

I had been invited to dinner with the Wrights—Charles, his wife, the photographer Holly Wright, and their son Luke, who had just been accepted at Sewanee and could tell us anything we wanted to know about computers. They live in a handsome Victorian house in Charlottesville. Their dining room has been converted from a parlor, and is large enough for a fireplace and grand piano. We sat at an eighteenth-century Sheraton walnut table. But the formality was offset by odd details—a witch ball, the bit from the horse of the infamous bandit Joaquin Murieta. Opposite my chair was an imposing oil portrait of Wright's great-grandfather, Charles Penzel, for whom the poet was named. Penzel, from minor Bohemian nobility, had emigrated to America at sixteen. No sooner had he settled down than the Civil War erupted. At twenty-three he took a bullet in the mouth as he yelled "Charge!" during the Battle of Chickamauga. After that tumultuous start, Penzel eventually became a banker in Little Rock, Arkansas, and even wrote poems. One, addressed to a war widow and printed up in a newspaper of the time, begins: "Beyond the flight of Time, / Beyond the reign of Death, / There surely is some better clime, / Where life is not a breath . . ."

After dinner we went up to Wright's huge attic study. It's kept obsessively neat—a trait, he says, he gets from his father, a civil engineer whose desk was scrupulously organized. Here is a poet for whom—as one looks around the room—arrangements matter. On one wall of shelves his books are arranged by their size, not by author or subject. In fact, there are fewer books than one might imagine, but more images: stacks of postcards, a zebra rug, gadgets, bird skulls, an heirloom sword—totems all. We pull up chairs next to what he calls his shelf of sacred texts, his lifelong masters, the voices that enabled him to find his own. There beside us are Dante, Pound, the Bible, Plath, Hemingway, Babel, Stevens, Williams, Crane, Roethke, Whitman, Dickinson, Rimbaud, Hopkins, Montale, an anthology of Chinese verse.

Across the room from us, in a narrow dormer alcove, is his desk with its Hermes portable typewriter. Above it are photographs of his wife and of Verona, taken during his first visit there in 1959. Beside these, a drawing of Campana, and a page from an old edition of *Inferno*, Canto XXIV. "What I look at has everything to do with what I think," he quickly explains.

Near the desk, at the end of a daybed, is what looks like an

old tin footlocker. Stencilled on the front of it is the name
H. W. Wilkinson. It rings a bell.]

May I ask what you keep in the box?

Of course. Family things, mostly. Old letters, land grant deeds
in Arkansas, a couple of family trees. That sort of stuff. Actu-
ally, the land grant deeds are interesting, one signed by James
K. Polk, one by John Quincy Adams, and one by Andrew
Jackson. Simpler presidencies in those days, when you could
spend time signing grants for the territory. The whole lot was
in a bottom drawer of my father's desk when he died and I've
just rather unceremoniously stuck it in this tin box I bought in
an antique shop in California. Family letters in almost indeci-
pherable hands from the mid-1800s in Arkansas, a couple of
documents from a great-aunt of mine tracing the family lines
on my father's side, from Maryland through Virginia to Ten-
nessee and finally to Arkansas. A lock of Robert E. Lee's hair,
if you can believe that! There are bunches of snapshots from
my childhood as well. And my old arrowhead collection I had
as a boy. And a skeleton or two—all the poems I wrote in Italy
when I was in the army, which I have vowed to throw away
every year since 1961, but haven't succeeded in doing yet.
And a diary of sorts I kept the first year I was in the army, in
California and Italy, before I began trying to write those po-
ems. Wretched stuff. Execrable stuff. I can't bring myself to
read it or throw it away. I'm going to do both soon. I guess I
keep thinking there might be something I can use one day.
But after all these years of ransacking that box for material, I
should know better. A kind of poetic *memento mori*, I suppose.

*And one of your great-grandfathers was a senator from Arkansas,
wasn't he?*

Oh, farther back than that. In the late 1830s—I don't know
how many "greats" that makes him. 1837 is the date of the
picture we have of the Senate chamber down in the dining
room. He's in it, along with Ambrose Sevier, the other senator

from Arkansas, and a distant relative. It's an interesting engraving—Longfellow is up in the balcony, as well as Audubon and the original Cassius Clay. His name was William Savin Fulton. I got the picture because no one else in the family wanted it. I suppose it is rather ugly, but I'm fond of it. He was the family's "illustrious ancestor." Most families have one back down the line, I guess. He's still known as Governor Fulton in the family, for some reason. I just used his recipe for eggnog at Christmas, it's a real killer. I don't know that much about him, really. I suppose there might be more in the box, in some of the letters, but the handwriting is difficult to read, and I'm not sure what else I *need* to know. Nothing, probably. He just shines back there, our distant star, whose name we all know, but not much else.

Now I remember. You dedicated The Southern Cross *to the same mysterious H. W. Wilkinson whose name is stencilled on that tin locker. It's meant, then—that dedication—as a gesture to your past? This trunk is really a sort of voice-box, a memory and a throat for the past. The poems in* The Southern Cross *have that character too.*

Mr. Wilkinson is as mysterious to me as he is to you. His name was on the box when I bought it, and that's all I know about him. *The Southern Cross* was dedicated to the box, actually, as you surmise, and not to Mr. Wilkinson per se: he's just a stand-in for a catch-all, if such a thing is possible. A voice-box is a nice way to put it, although it's been more so in the past than it is now. Especially around the time of *Bloodlines* and, as you say, *The Southern Cross.* I used some of its material also in "Arkansas Traveller," from *The Other Side of the River.* My great-grandfather's obituary from the Little Rock paper in 1906, some fragments from the letters about the move from Tennessee to Arkansas in the early 1800s. Stuff like that. I guess I thought it was cute, as well, to dedicate a book ostensibly to someone I didn't know. But, as you say, the real gesture was to my past, a way of letting those speak whose voices are too faint to hear. So it's a voice-box in that sense, too; it amplifies the deep and desperate whispers of those who have disappeared into a kind of request for recognition. Sort of like La Pia in Canto V of the *Purgatorio*, though in no way so poignant or affecting: "*Deh, quando tu sarai tornato al mondo / e riposato de la lunga via / . . . recorditi di me, che son La Pia . . .*" "Remember me, remember me . . ." Well, I hope that some of the poems in which I use their leftovers do remember them. And the first poem in *The Southern Cross*, "Homage to Paul Cézanne," takes up that charge somewhat—though the dead are not named, I did have my own family, from the box, in mind. "A throat for the past." That's a nice way of putting it.

You've mentioned your early poems. Is it nostalgia that makes you keep them? What are they like? Or better, what did they know and not know how to do?

They didn't know how to do *anything*. Mostly, I guess, because they didn't know what they were *supposed* to do. And I myself had no clue. I had read *The Pisan Cantos* and *The Selected Poems of Ezra Pound*. So I started at the end instead of the beginning, trying to write about what I was seeing—Italy—in terms of what I had been reading—*Pisan Cantos*. Wrong from the start—an Attic disgrace. If one has to write poorly before one can write well—which I think is true—and if that can be extended to read that one has to write deplorably before one can write extraordinarily well, then I definitely started in the right place for the latter. I suppose it's nostalgia that makes me keep them. That and the sense of duty that one shouldn't destroy one's stunted darlings. Keep them out of sight, yes, but don't abuse them. Rather like the retarded great-aunt in the attic, that mainstay of Southern gothic. Soon, I know, I must harden my heart and dispose of them. Euthanasia, so to speak. But for the moment, to continue your figure from the last question, they lie there like a bone in the dark throat of my past. It's not their fault. They just never had a chance.

Even with those early poems, it seems a bit of a late start. You were already in the army, weren't you? Why then—or rather, why not before then?

Why I didn't before then is unanswerable, probably. Who knows why we don't do things? I would imagine it was because poetry was never presented to me in a way that generated any excitement. I certainly remember nothing of it either in boarding school or in college. In college, in fact, there was one creative writing course taught every other year by the Shakespeare professor—not exactly a commitment on the school's part. And all the straight English courses I took seemed to revolve around prose, not poetry. An ongoing debility, I might add, almost everywhere. It didn't help, I suppose, that I was a history major as well. I did try to write stories in college, or what I thought were stories—mood pieces, really, purple prose on the model of Thomas Wolfe. I had no idea *how* to do anything, and no one told me or showed me. If I had been a photograph, I would have been underexposed and underdeveloped. As it was, I was merely undereducated. But then, my college never claimed it was in the business of turning out writers—William Styron, for instance, left after his freshman year. It turned out lawyers, doctors, and Presbyterian ministers. At least back in those days it did. It wasn't until I stumbled onto *The Selected Poems of Ezra Pound* that I discovered a form that seemed suited to my mental and emotional inclinations—the lyric poem, a form, or subgenre, I guess, that didn't depend on a narrative structure, but on an imagistic one, an associational one. "Gists and piths," as they say, instead of intricacy of narrative line.

Okay, but why then? What took?

That's a bit easier. Mostly it's because I read a poem that just overwhelmed me, blew me away, as the saying goes. It was "Blandula, Tenulla, Vagula" by Pound, from the *Selected Poems.* I loved the sound of it—it was in iambic pentameter, although I didn't know it at the time, and even if I had, I wouldn't have known what that was. That it was describing the very location I was reading it in—Sirmione peninsula, in the ruins of the villa of the Roman poet, Catullus—didn't hurt either. In any case, it was enough of a thunderclap to move me swiftly through the *Selected Poems,* and farther down the road as well. I bought a Guanda paperback edition of *The Pisan Cantos,* recently translated into Italian with the original English on the facing page, and read that. Understanding almost nothing, I might add, except some place names. Pound had, a year before—this was in 1959—returned to Italy and was living above Merano, in Brunnenberg, so his books were available at the local bookstores. At least they were available in Verona, where I lived. Later I got a Faber & Faber *Cantos,* and bought *Rock Drill* and *Thrones,* too. But it was *The Pisan Cantos* that struck me, along with *Cathay* in the *Selected Poems.* It was the first poetry I ever bought. I was twenty-three. Anyway, that's why then, finally, I began to try to write poems.

You say you began writing in Italy. You could as easily say you began writing in the army—but you don't.

Well, being in the army is physical, being in Italy is metaphysical. Or so it seemed at the time. So you could say, and I often do, that I began writing poems in the army in Italy. The metaphysics of the quotidian. The army, actually, was very good to me, much better to me than I was to it. I gave them four years of my time and they gave me back, it turned out, a life. The army was only the base, as Stevens says, but it *was* the base. And from it I drifted into the Italian landscape and was never the same again. I never *looked* at anything the same way again. I never *listened* to anything in the same way. My eight-to-five in the army was the old way, the rest of the time was the new way. And since I never wrote poems, or what I thought of as poems, during army hours, I suppose I tend to think of my writing as being in Italy, off-duty, as opposed to the army workaday world. The army was still the United States—off-duty was a foreign country. The army was fact, Italy was fiction. Again, the metaphysics of the quotidian. Or, poetry is the fiction we use to prove the fact. Something like that.

What did Pound contribute, and what did Italy prompt—or can you separate them now?

Pound contributed *Cathay* to listen to and *The Pisan Cantos* to look at. Conversational tone in a high mode in the former, emotional road maps in the latter. Italy prompted a realignment with the world and its attendant possibilities. Actually, I suppose it goes a bit further than that. Which is to say, if form imposes and structure allows, then Pound imposed and Italy allowed. Reading Pound showed me there was a way to do what I had always wanted to do—to write—and Italy somehow allowed me to do it. I don't quite know how. Aiding and abetting, I guess. The same continuous sense of discovery everywhere I turned in the country that lay everywhere I turned in the books. I can separate them, of course, but the way you separate a glove from a hand. Or a skin from a snake. Still, Pound was a temporary obsession, a jump-start, as it were. Italy has continued in me to this day. A major battery, as it were. It has given me more than landscape, however. Montale and Campana, for instance, not to mention our main man, Dott. Alighieri. Morandi and all the painters. The fact is that I discovered, in a way, each through the other, and during the early days it *was* difficult to separate them. Now, though, to finish the image off, the glove is in the dresser but the hand goes on about its business. As for the snake, the less said about that the better.

By the way, did you ever meet Pound while you were there?

Actually, I never did. I came close once, in 1969, when I was living in Venice and teaching at the University of Padua. Jim Tate was visiting me and we arranged, through a mutual friend of mine and Olga Rudge's, Vittoria Cozzi, for the three of us—Vittoria, Jim, and me—to call on Pound on a particular Monday. This was on a Wednesday, I think. Well, between Wednesday and Monday, Pound got a call about his honorary degree from Hamilton College and was already in the States by the time our appointment came around. It was his last trip to America, it turned out. Otherwise, I used to see him taking his walks along the Zattere off and on. I used to see him and Olga in Piazza San Marco before they left for San Ambrogio for the winter. He, as I recall, always wore (at least when I saw him) a beautiful camel's hair topcoat and a muffler. And a hat. He always wore a hat. I would see him occasionally, always with Miss Rudge, through the window at the odd restaurant. I remember wanting, early on, back when I was in the army, to go up to Brunnenberg to see him. We used to have maneuvers outside Merano, and Brunnenberg was close by—or relatively so. All this, of course, was just so much fantasy. You must remember that I hadn't even published a book and that Pound didn't speak. The closest I ever came was when I stood anonymously next to him under the porticoes of San Marco, looking at the church and the piazza one evening. But what was there to say? "I like your poems." "Is this the city of Dioce?" Besides, it was, in the end, the best thing, wasn't it? Standing side by side with him, looking at the most beautiful square in the world, in the city he taught me to look at in ways that would change my life. Water and silence. Some words, I guess, are better left unuttered. Or so they say.

Let's stay in Italy a moment longer, but jump ahead across the years. It seems to me that in your most recent book, as in your earliest, Italy is a kind of sacred place for you—almost a motherland, while America is your fatherland. And of course you've translated Montale and Campana. Can you tell me—can you even tell yourself—what that landscape and culture have meant to you?

Well, *Zone Journals* is about sacred places. Sacred places, language and landscape, and how they coexist in each other, and speak for, and to, each other. The two primary sacred places in the book are the Long Island of the Holston River in Kingsport, Tennessee, where I grew up, sacred ceremonial ground of the Cherokee nation, and northern Italy, especially the Veneto region, where I first began writing poems. The center, the exact center of the *Journals,* takes place during a two-month period spent in a farmhouse outside Padua in the summer of 1985, with my family and Mark Strand and his family. The center of the center, as it were, is a description of a room of Renaissance frescoes in the Palazzo Schifanoia in Ferrara. They depict the tripartite levels of existence—everyday life, allegorical life, and ideal life. It's a concept that appeals to me.

Anyway, yes, that part of Italy does have "sacred place" status for me. As does language itself, the most sacred place of all. And since my own sense of language was stumbled upon in Italy, I suppose that does make it a kind of motherland, place of rebirth and nurture, let's say, for pomposity's sake.

As for what that landscape and culture have meant to me, it's obvious I can't say. For over twenty-five years I've been trying to do so, but I keep coming up short and having to try again. I'll probably keep at it until the end, and come a cropper all the way. But the very least I *can* say is that it completely restructured my way of looking at the world, it reordered dramatically the list of what is important to me in life, and it reshuffled forever my ambitions. Not an unnoticeable change. Its landscape has become the inner landscape I walk through, its paintings and literature—especially Montale and Campana, as you mention, and Dante as well—have become intellectual touchstones for me. It did, in the end, what any conversion does for you—it makes the scales drop from your eyes, and it changes your name.

Then you returned to the States in 1961 and enrolled at the Iowa Writers' Workshop. What was it like in those days?

It was much smaller then, about half the size it is now, and it hadn't reached the apotheosizic state it seems to dwell in these days. It had run through only one group of poets, basically, who were to become well-known—the Justice-Levine-Snodgrass bunch. It was probably better known for its past teachers—Lowell, Berryman, Paul Engle—than for its students. It had had Flannery O'Connor in fiction, of course. It had just finished its first twenty-five years. Also, it was its own entity, funded out of Paul Engle's pocket and what he could wheedle out of Quaker Oats in Cedar Rapids and Iowa Power and Light. Now it's part of the English Department proper, with a huge budget and giant money from the James Michener Foundation. The jewel in the crown, as it were. And they've run a lot more people through it in the twenty-five years just past than they did in the first twenty-five. But it was a wonderful place for me. As I say, I'd never studied poetry as such, knew nothing about the writing of it, didn't even know what an iambic pentameter line was, had read nothing but Pound and Eliot and some Montale and Campana in Italian. Every page in my book was blank. I was twenty-six in 1961 when I arrived, and had never written a proper poem in my life. The workshop itself was housed in a group of Quonset huts left over from the time of World War II—there is a parking lot, without plaque, I might add, where they used to be. I was very lucky in having some wonderful classmates who taught me what and how to read, and what and how to write. Mark Strand, primarily, and Al Lee and William Brown. Neither Brown nor Lee write any more, but they were extremely talented and helped me enormously in the early days. Strand still does. Donald Justice was our teacher and controlled the entire technical and moral fiber of the workshop. He was exemplary in all ways. I probably learned more from him than anyone else who ever went through his classes. I was absorbent and soaked up whatever spilled out in the class-rooms, in the bars after classes, in the offices, everywhere. Oh, I had so much to learn. And by the time I left, I did know what an iambic pentameter line was.

An amazing winter—at least by my standards—also led to the hot-house effect that the workshop had back then. We had twenty-five inches of snow on the ground by December first and didn't see the ground again until March. During one stretch of several weeks, the temperature never got above zero. God, it was cold. Nothing to do but read and write. Nowhere to go but indoors. As I say, I probably got more out of my two years there than anyone else who ever went. Even my Montale translations started there. I loved it.

What about writing workshops? You have studied in them, taught in them—and over the years, no doubt, have seen them change.

Actually, they haven't changed much, I think. At least not the ones I've had any connection with. Perhaps the students have changed—and I think they have, a great deal—but the work-shops themselves are still the same process of give and take. More take than give, usually. I'm talking about from the writer's side. From the teacher's side, it's trying to give what the poem wants. More often than not, you tend to give more than the poem can take, both positively and negatively. Or more than the poem deserves. It can, of course, be very beneficial. I know of very few cases where it is destructive—and then only because of other, outside factors. I think it can be neutral, neither helpful nor harmful. But on the whole, I have found them to do what they should do—encourage the talented and discourage the not-so-talented.

I am, as I think I have intimated, almost a 100 percent product of the writing workshop system. And it was not only good for me, but necessary as well. I'm talking about graduate workshops now. The one I attended stood in for all the early writing guidance I never had, and saved me years of floundering and fooling myself that I knew what I was about when, in fact, I hadn't a clue. But not everyone was, or is, in my predicament. In fact, nowadays, almost no one is. In a sense, the original battle the workshop system had to fight, the lack of undergraduate writing instruction, has been won, and students come to the graduate programs already in possession of what we had only after a two-year graduate stint. The undergraduate departments have been almost totally infiltrated. Every campus has its poet and its fiction writer. The graduate programs now tend to be rather like feedlots or holding pens. Productive, perhaps, but maybe not wholly necessary. Still, there seems to be a market for them.

Could we say that workshops help the apprentice poet make the inevitable mistakes—and realize them—more quickly?

Certainly undergraduate workshops do. I think they are marvelous courses, as I tried to say just now—they seem to me to be pertinent components of any undergraduate English department curriculum. It's only the graduate workshops that I am of two minds about. Any undergraduate student who takes a workshop, whether he can write a lick or not, is a better student for the time he has spent there. A better reader and, one can hope, a better writer. You can't beat that. Now if he is one of the two or three every five years who may actually turn out to *be* a writer, so much the better for everyone all around. The same probably holds true for the graduate workshops as well, though the students seem less willing to make the mistakes. There is still much for them to learn, but too often they don't seem to want to learn it. They are still conserving what they learned as undergraduates and all too often seem willing to hole up in that accomplishment without trying to break through into another zone of contemplation, say, or further center of attention. Graduate workshops should be just as adventurous and abyss-jumping as undergraduate ones. Too often, lately, it seems to me that the students don't want to make the mistakes they need to make. It's as though the workshop were the end of something and not a pre-beginning. Hemingway said, "What you win in Boston you lose in Chicago." Too many students don't want to play in Chicago, win or lose. But if you don't lose in Chicago, you can't win in Boston. So you gotta play.

When you pick up a new book of poems—a book by someone else, I mean—what do you look for first?

Hmmm . . . Music and substance, I guess, as most anyone would. One man's music, naturally, is another man's Muzak. One's ear is one's Virgil, however, leading you on. It's difficult, though, the older you get. You're harder and harder to satisfy. Meters become monotonous, measures become minimal, or nonexistent. You keep harking back to the great dead, as Dylan Thomas called them, and asking where their like are. And, of course, their like are in the tomb. *"Mais où sont les neiges d'antan?"* Not a good question to ask. One looks for a reach, an ambition. One looks for language, an exuberance. Well, one looks for Hart Crane and Emily Dickinson, for Ezra Pound and Walt Whitman. There seem to me to be certain absolutes in whatever field of endeavor one is in. In business and banking they may be availability and convertibility, security and safekeeping, minimal loss and steady, incremental accession. I don't think it's that way in poetry, though such values will get you to temporary high places. Brilliance is what you reach for, language that has a life of its own, seriousness of subject matter beyond the momentary gasp and glitter, a willingness to take on what's difficult and beautiful, a willingness to be different and abstract, a willingness to put on the hair shirt and go into the desert and sit still, and listen hard, and write it down, and tell no one . . . Is that asking too much? Probably. Is there going to be someone to come along who fits this description? Probably. Will we recognize him when he comes? Probably not.

In fact, how often do you find these qualities? Or any of them separately?

Not often, obviously. Very seldom, in fact. But there are other, more minor virtues and felicities to comfort one. And in my own generation there are poets who I think incorporate some if not all of the major qualities I look for. Writers like Mark Strand and Charles Simic, C. K. Williams and Louise Glück and James Tate. I think Michael Palmer is onto something as well. There are many talented younger writers now, probably more than ever before, but I do find a caution among them that is more pervasive than one would like, a timidity about taking on something outside themselves, outside their reach. Jorie Graham tries a real reach, and I admire her for that. And there are some others. The problem with all of us as we get older is that we begin writing as though we were somebody. One should always write as if one were nobody, for that's what we are. In the giant shadow of Dante's wing, for instance, we are nobody and should never forget it. So we should always write out of our ignorance and desire and ambition, never out of some sense of false well-being, some tinge of success. There is no success in poetry, there is only the next inch, the next handhold out of the pit.

The subtitle of your Country Music *is* Selected Early Poems. *At the time, you had four books to select from. How did you go about it? By 1982, when* Country Music *appeared, your sense of a poem—and of your own poems especially—must have changed a great deal from what it had been twenty years before, when your first poems were published. Which of them still seemed valuable?*

To start with, I eliminated everything from my first book, *The Grave of the Right Hand,* except for the five prose poems that I used as a kind of "proem" to the larger structure I had been working on for about seven years, a trilogy of books—*Hard Freight, Bloodlines,* and *China Trace*—that was sort of a past, present, and future, an autobiography by fragmental accretion, as it were. Books—and poems—about family, childhood, landscape, and place. And one, *China Trace,* about the future, a spiritual future. The trilogy also had a structural progression, from a book of disparate, individual lyrics, through one of sequences and ending with a book-length poem—granted, an odd one, but one that has a character who goes from the first poem, where he shrugs off childhood, to the last, where he ends up a constellation in the heaven of the fixed stars— not enough belief to be able to get beyond what he can see, into the empyrean. Each poem is a chapter in the book, the book a little "pilgrim's progress"—with a small *p.* What interested me then—and what still interests me when I have to think about it—was the accumulation of the three books, and not individual poems. Although I still have a fondness for "Skins" and "Tattoos" as poems, as well as for *China Trace.* Nothing actually seems "valuable," although some things, including those, seem retrievable. And even though each book one writes is in essence an apprentice volume, *The Grave of the Right Hand* was my major apprentice volume, so I was glad to be able to rescue anything from it. Thom Gunn once said to me that you'll like your first book much better as you get older. I've found that not to be the case for me. Which is, I suppose, the answer to part of your question—when I first started writing, I was interested in the tight weave of the surface only—technique as a statement in itself, so to speak. I no longer, in 1982, or now in 1988, believed this. Technique is half a statement in itself. It's a subject without a verb or object. As I went along, my books, I hope, started to reflect this. My interest in technical matters, the "how," has not lessened, but my interest in what I am trying to say, the "what," has become more than equal to it. Like a spider's web that is tight in its individual parts, but expandable in its larger structure, the entire poem trembles when any area is touched. Its meaning is almost invisible, but can be mortal to the right being. Or the wrong one.

When you read through your early books today, do you have the sense of encountering a distinctive "Charles Wright" style in them?

It depends on how far back you go. Before a poem called "Dog Creek Mainline" in *Hard Freight,* no; after it, yes. Which is to say, for the first ten years of my serious writing, no. It's odd, though, that I recognize more of what I'm trying to do now in stuff I wrote *before* I went to Iowa, when I knew *nothing,* than in the stuff I wrote between 1961 and 1971. The early stuff, as I've explained, wasn't any good—in fact, it was bloody awful— but the *impulse* was there, the reach and horizon were there.

Style is very important to me, actually. As far as I can see, there is no great art without great style, however sophisticated or unsophisticated it might be. All major writers are great stylists. Even Faulkner, in his way. It's too bad the term has come to be pejorative—all style, no substance. On the contrary. Major style usually, if not always, signals real substance. It's hard to think of anyone, from Hemingway to Yeats to Pound to Crane, of the major Moderns who wasn't a great stylist. And it isn't, of course, restricted to this century. I yearn to have a significant style. I want people to be able to look at a poem of mine on the page, read it, and to say, as though they had seen a painting on a wall, "This is Charles Wright."

I sometimes think I can recognize one. And that's as much for what's been left out—a lot of discursive stuffing and expressionistic uphol-stery that clutters so much contemporary poetry—as for what's been included. There's a sound, a sweet-and-sour melody. There's a look, a jagged elegance. There's a pace, the jump-cuts and loping back. And above all, an ambition. Isn't that a part of style too?

Well, yes, of course. But most of those, taken in the abstract, are surface. Except for the last one, the one that sends roots down and makes the thing take hold. And transforms the other three into more than meets the eye. Or ear. I mean, there is style, and there is Style. When everything clicks, style *is* Style, everything inextricably bound up in language and its ambitions, everything palpable in the *is*ness, the radiance that language offers. It's a concentration of the particular, I suppose, despite the gravity of the general. Transcendence inside its own skin. In other words, it tends to be not just how you write, but what you write as well, and why you write it. I feel about style the way Heidegger felt about being. It's inside, not outside. All those things you mention—sound and look and, what was it, pacing? and ambition, all have to come from an inner necessity, a "thereness," a *haeccitas,* that makes you write as you do. Jazz, for example, may be all style, but it's all soul as well. Everything that we see comes from something that we don't see. *Duende* or *dharma* or *Dasein,* it all comes down to the same thing, you are what you are, and what you are in that secret place is what you write. Well, it's complicated, isn't it, and I haven't expressed myself very well. Clarity. Faith, hope, and clarity. Some things are more difficult to clarify than others, aren't they? Great clarity is great style, however hard it may be.

In Bloodlines *you began to write sequences of poems, and that impulse toward length, juxtaposition, complexity, a layering of voices and memories, has marked each of your books since. What is it in that kind of poem that attracts you?*

All the things you mention, I guess—length, juxtaposition, complexity, and layering. Especially juxtaposition and layering. Voices and memory. Actually, in *Bloodlines* and *China Trace,* though there is an extension of the understructure—sequences in one, and the other being a long poem, now in forty-six parts—the surface weave is a continual tightening, winding it down as tight as I can make it. Again, the spider's web—the web gets bigger, but the pattern gets tighter and smaller. Beginning with *The Southern Cross,* I set about unwinding the whole apparatus, and it gets increasingly loose through *The Other Side of the River* and into *Zone Journals.*

Montale said that all poetry rises out of prose and yearns to return to it. That sounds right to me. And the interesting place to work in is that yearning, between the two power points. Perhaps all poetry aspires toward the condition not of music, but of the prose poem. Another reason I got into lengthier gestures and juxtapositional organization was that I thought I had taken the lyric as far as I could in tightening it in *China Trace*. Relaxation seemed a good idea at the time. And that was about the time I began to look closely at Cézanne and Morandi, two painters who used space and structure in ways that appealed to me. I've tried to carry some of those ideas over into my poems. So, structural considerations, architecture in the poem, the use of space, design. The temporal surface, or the attempt to make a temporal surface that was extra-temporal, continued, of course, as it had always been—the first obsession. Not necessarily the greater but still the first. What attracted me? Amplitude, desire, the ventriloquism of the past.

Is that true for Zone Journals *as well? They seem more relaxed, more expansive than the earlier sequences.*

I think so. They are verse journals, remember, and are greatly concerned with line as well as story line. They are, I suppose, in as loose a form as I can work with and still work in lines. As opposed to sentences, I mean. One of the purposes of the journals was to work with a line that was pushed as hard as I could push it toward prose, conversational in tone but with the rhythmic concentration of what we call poetry. The journals' very nature, by definition, makes them more explicit. They are more didactic than other poems, perhaps, and more emotionally open. One tends to speak one's mind more nakedly in journals. One tends to say what is really troubling one's sleep. At the same time, of course, they *are* poems, with all a poem's avoidances and exclusions. Still, the word "journal" is operative, and allows more quotidiana in, and the speculations such dailiness leads to.

One more thing. Some years ago Octavio Paz called for what I seem to remember as a "Baroque-abstract" in painting. A kind of Mannerism. A non-pejorative Mannerism. I think that has happened in the work, say, of Frank Stella. I think it is also happening, here and there, in poetry. One could name names—Ashbery, for instance. It is a position that interests me as well.

Let me go back to The Southern Cross. *The splendid title poem of that book sets out, in a crucial sense, to be a very personal poem, but isn't by any means a conventionally autobiographical one. Autobiography seems central but intermittent in your poems. Is that a fair estimate?*

I think so. In fact, that's a splendid way of putting it. Central because it's always there, intermittent because it doesn't always show. Rather like the progression of the story lines in the poems themselves—central but intermittently in evidence. A submerged narrative, as it were. A kind of minus tide that runs just under everything and adds by subtraction. Anyone's autobiography, at least in his own eyes, is made up of a string of luminous moments, numinous moments. It's a necklace we spend our lives assembling. That's what "The Southern Cross" is about, saying some of those beads. But that "I" isn't *I* anymore. It's someone else, the character who plays me, someone who's a better actor than I could ever be. I'm just the writer. Someone else is starring in my part. I remember him just well enough to try to write about him. A case of the negative sublime. I guess art's always after the fact. The real is imaginary, or imagined. Reconstitution, reconstruction, representation is all we're left with. Autobiography becomes biography in the end.

As a Southern poet, you might be expected to favor a broadly narrative poetry. Though you've called some poems "Stories" or "Journals," in general you shy from straight narrative. Why is that?

It's simple, really. I can't tell a story. Only Southerner I know who can't. And, in truth, I have no real interest in telling one. The point of telling a story is the telling; the story itself is not the point. I always wanted to get to the end and find out what the point was. Still do.

Let's talk for a minute about how you put a poem together. It seems to me that an apt metaphor for one of your completed poems is the X ray rather than the statue. I mean, a reader can see through its verbal "finish," back to those memories that float as they do first in the mind, as images. *Is that what starts a poem going for you—a cluster of images?*

It does, actually. Perhaps not a cluster. One would do. Something I see, usually; something observed. The "little dropped hearts" of the camellia blooms scattered under the huge camellia bush in my backyard in Laguna Beach fifteen years ago started the poem "Tattoos." And since "Tattoos" begat "Skins," you could say that those fallen blossoms were the beginning of the entire book, *Bloodlines,* as the other eight poems went in to accentuate or ameliorate the two long central ones. Of course, each one had its own separate trigger, but the initial pull was off the dropped blossoms. For example, "Skins" began not with an image but with a phrase, "there comes a time when what you are is what you will be." Then it went on from there. In the old days, when I was starting out—say 1959 to 1969—my poems almost always began with a rhythm, a little wordless riff I'd hear in my head. Then I'd try to fill in the blanks, even with nonsense words, if I had to, to get it down. I suppose it was because I was learning, or trying to learn, the meters—syllabics, accentuals, accentual-syllabics, and so forth. I always had these things going around in my head. There was a period when I almost thought in pentameter, and a period when every time I concentrated on something it developed into a seven-syllable line. After a while, after I came to be easier with these meters, if not at ease with them, my attention became more visual, and what I would see would begin to cluster, to use your word, around a sound pattern. When I began to work exclusively in free verse, around 1970, the images began to develop their own rhythms, I suppose, as they aggregated. Still, it's always been rhythm and image for me, as opposed to, say, ideas, that get a poem going. Mark Strand, for example, works from ideas, I'd imagine. I think very few of his poems begin with something observed. Observed physically, I mean. I often wish I were more like that myself, as I feel somewhat restricted. But I'm not. Which isn't to say an idea or two doesn't work its way in, but my poems don't start with one.

How does memory fit into that kind of scheme?

Well, memories . . . Hmmm. I suppose memory would be the invisible end of a vanishing rope, and the thing observed would be the visible end. Memory is the subjective correlative, to adopt, or adapt, the Reverend Mr. Eliot's vocabulary, of the seen object, and your job is to turn the equation around, to make the unseen seen. Instead of emotional equivalents, they become visual responses. The focus is on the *unseen,* and how these things are brought up into view through the unemotional lens of the tactile present. I don't know. I do like your metaphor of my poems being more like X rays than statues, though. Revealing that which is hidden, unseen but not forgotten. Showing its relationship and necessity to the working organism of the present. The memories may float in the mind, but they are fixed in their functioning places in the body of the poem. This is beginning to sound like a lot of mumbo jumbo to me. Theories always come after the poems. Theories are always secondary, no matter how intriguing we make them, or how compelling. Theories are easy. It's the poems that are difficult.

And how do you know when a poem is, in fact, done?

When I feel a theory about it coming on.

Seriously, how do you know, if you do know?

It used to be easy, as a matter of fact. In the old days—the old days are pre–*The Southern Cross*, all the early poems collected in *Country Music*—when I was more interested in the traditional, self-contained lyric, I'd know it when I got to the end, as I knew where, and what, the end was. And, in fact, I'd often start with the end, a last line or a last image, and work down to it. More recently, in the past ten to eleven years, it hasn't been that easy. If the poems nowadays are at all self-contained and boxlike, they are like Chinese boxes, boxes within boxes. But more often they are too encompassing to be analogous even to that. Something like, for instance, "A Journal of the Year of the Ox" would be more like an aircraft carrier—many small lyrics riding on its superstructure. How's that for an outrageous linkage? Of course the "Ox" poem had to finish at the end of December, 1985, as one of its structures was the length of the year. But what went in, and what ended it, was very open. When I thought, or felt, the circle had almost been completed, I stopped. The same with the earlier poem, "The Southern Cross," which relied so much on memory, or on my inability to remember. When I thought I had not remembered enough, and that some Neoplatonic, neocircle was almost complete, I stopped. Of course, I then went back and cut out over one hundred and forty lines, which seemed to me mere incidents and not true detail. If God lives in the detail, as Flaubert tells us, then only the incidental lives in the incident. You've got to be careful to distinguish between them. I guess there is more feel than formula as to where a poem ends now for me. It's probably never finished in the old sense, but just over. And given their more elaborate, incremental structures, that's probably a good thing. Or at least not a bad thing.

Because you've published excerpts from it, I know you keep a notebook. Do you mine it regularly for poems, or does it have a distinct life, a different purpose?

It's not exactly a notebook, not in the usual sense. It's a crossbreed, really, a combination commonplace book and jotting book. It has no narrative structure or ultimate purpose. Most of what goes into it has to do with poetics or ideas on art in general. The last thing I put in it was a couple of days ago, something about narrative and the image. Wait a minute, it's right over there, I'll get it. Here it is: "Narrative does not dictate the image; the image dictates the narrative." That sort of thing. Here's another: "One of the differences between poetry and prose is that—good or bad—lines are final. Sentences are never final, but are ceaselessly rearrangeable." Well, one could go on. I don't, as a matter of fact, mine it for poems, as you can imagine from those two examples. I used to write in it a lot more before I embarked on the *Journals*. Since part of the scaffolding of the *Journals* is process itself, and ideas about that process, I've been able, from time to time, to work those ideas into the texts themselves. It's especially apparent in "March Journal," for instance. Anyway, to answer your question, I suppose it does have a distinct life, or half-life, such as it is. It certainly has a different purpose. It's an escape valve for pronouncements to myself. You can hear it hissing over there if you listen hard enough.

Your poems have struck some readers as spacey, the work of a free-floating, delicately dissociated sensibility. And some of your effects, I'll confess, are eerily like pipe dreams. Have drugs played a role?

That's what Hopkins said about Keats, sort of. Wait a minute. I put it in my "London Journal"—I mean my "English Journal." Let's see. Here, it's the first stanza of Keats's birthday entry: "Hopkins thought your verse abandoned itself / To an enervating luxury, a life of impressions / In Fairyland, life of a dreamer / And lacking the manly virtues of active thought." No pun intended, I suppose. And that from someone who practically hyperventilated on the Lord! Was Keats a laudanum-head? Not that I've heard. Maybe a drop here and there, but no De Quincey he. It's funny. I just reread *The Confessions of an English Opium Eater* last summer. Pretty good stuff for a junkie. Not to mention *The English Mail Coach*, which is even better. Well, I never thought of the effects, some of the effects, in my poems as, what did you say, "spacey"? Or like pipe dreams, a word whose origin I've just seen for the first time. Opium pipe, right? Hmmm . . . your question. Drugs have played almost no role whatsoever in my work. Certainly not at all when compared to someone like Rimbaud or Nerval, poets I admire greatly. Or even poets whose work I admire somewhat, like Allen Ginsberg, for instance. No role at all. Still, I have smoked some dope in my day. And I've drunk a little whiskey. And I've done some coke, as the saying goes. And only in one case has it had any physical effect on a given poem. I learned early on that I, in any case, had to separate the drug and the word. It was especially depressing when I was in my Rimbaud phase. I felt a total failure. The problem was I couldn't drink and concentrate—unlike, I understand,

Faulkner could and Hart Crane could—and I couldn't smoke pot and concentrate. At least not on writing. I could certainly concentrate on nothing or nothing's trappings with a fierce intensity. The main problem always seemed to be that I wanted to have fun, and writing wasn't fun. It was work. So I smoked dope and giggled. I drank whiskey and wine and brooded, which was fun. When I was writing *China Trace*, back in the mid-1970s, I tooted some cocaine after supper one night, went into the back yard on Oak Street back in Laguna, stared at the sky and then went into the little shack out there I used as a study and wrote a poem in ten or fifteen minutes. I was amazed. Total concentration, total focus and magnification. I was even more stunned the next day when I realized I didn't have to change a thing. I published it just the way I wrote it that night. It scared the hell out of me and I never tried it again. Ever. I realized that if I did it a second time, or so I thought at the time, I'd have to use coke every time I tried to write. So much for the rational disordering of the senses. I couldn't have afforded to write poems if cocaine was to be one of their ingredients. In fact, it was soon after that I stopped doing it altogether because it just got too expensive. Fortunately for me. I kept on smoking marijuana for some years, late at night, mostly, to go to sleep, but I've given that up too now. All I've got left is a dollop of Scotch at night and a little white wine. I never did LSD or mescaline, but did some peyote in the old days. Maybe it's that my senses are disordered most of the time anyhow, and my job is to rationalize them as much as possible. And when I slip, or don't do the job properly, the poems seem "spacey" and "free-floating." I've tried to anchor them as much as I could. I see no inherent virtue in ether.

There's a story to be told about pot and your whole generation of poets, no?

I suppose there is, though probably not by me. If, as Stevens said, "The book of moonlight has not been written yet," or something like that, surely the book of marijuana has not been written yet either. I guess what I'm trying to say is that there was more to the evolution of American Surrealism in the late 1960s and early 1970s than just an injection of Spanish poetry from the 1930s and Pablo Neruda and César Vallejo. They *were*, let's get this straight, the foundation and the "ark of the covenant," so to speak. But they also gave an artistic license or, better, an artistic alibi for the age. Nothing out of Breton was more surreal than watching tanks carrying dead and bleeding bodies, easing through the supper hour as millions swallowed the image along with their Hamburger Helper. The young poets were mirrors of the times, not the precursors. I think it's interesting that American Surrealism's high-water mark was about a ten-year period, say 1965 to 1975, whose other high-water marks were found in marijuana smoking and the Vietnam War. And although, in many ways, all three are with us still, they have either been absorbed into the culture—Surrealism into the mainstream of American poetry, marijuana into the mainstream of American drug abuse—or else the culture has grown around it, like a tree grows around an axe-head left in its trunk. Vietnam and the American body politic. Drugs and poetry have always gone together, from earliest shamanism up to the *Yage Letters* and on. It's not often that an entire generation gets involved in the practice, though, and I think that's what did happen, in varying degrees with various poets, in the time we're talking about. Was it a good thing? Remains to be seen. It certainly loosened up a lot of so-called academic writers, and that's not bad. Unlike Dada, which never got absorbed, or the current Language poetries, which I also think won't be absorbed—I imagine they both will remain as "examples," "exhibits," apart and behind glass—Surrealism seems to have found its own current in the pluralistic American stream of poetic consciousness. If pot helped that along, far out!

I guess what I really wanted to ask is a question about your daily routine—if there is one. Do you schedule your writing, or does it come in desultory bursts?

I used to have a routine—for years I wrote in the afternoon, unlike anyone else I've ever heard of. When I was in Italy I translated Montale in the morning, and twenty years later, in 1983, I did it again when I was working on the Campana. But that makes it sound as though I had a fixed routine, certain hours when I did certain things. And I don't have any such thing. And never did except for the hour-and-a-half it takes me to read the newspaper each morning. Of course there's B.C. and A.D.—Before Child and After Delivery. The past eighteen years have been much different from the nine before that. And certainly better, I might add. The beginnings of my little experiments with dislocation and discontinuity, the abstracting of the story line, all took place out of necessity in my case. Time was grabbed when grabbable, what with teaching, family, and all the other emanations bidding for its services. Innovation was the child of necessity for me. My poems became, or started to become, disconsecutive, going from stanza to stanza as units rather than from beginning to end as a seamless piece. Later, in *The Southern Cross, The Other Side of the River,* and *Zone Journals,* I tended to make an aesthetic of such impulses, and to widen them. All of which really doesn't answer your question, does it?

No, but it answers another question, and I'll ask it in just a minute. But first, let's get back to the business of your schedule, and if you have one.

No, I never did have a schedule, though I was chipping away at things rather consistently. When I *was* working on something, I worked on it every chance I got, morning, afternoon, or evening. So work *would* come in bursts, but not desultory ones. For instance, on "A Journal of the Year of the Ox," I seemed to be working every day that year. Obsessively. Of course, I tend to think about writing obsessively even when I don't have a project. I'd *like* to be writing all the time. I seldom read novels any more because I don't want to get caught up in something that might take me three to four days, or longer, away from thinking about poems. This hardly becomes justifiable when I go, as I have done, three months or longer between poems. But one must protect one's standards, mustn't one? For a highly organized person, as I am, my writing schedule is wholly erratic.

Now let's circle back to the answer you were giving just before. You were talking about a new kind of poem you started writing—a poem of impulses, of disconnected stanzas linked by association. That gravitates toward the short poem, and our literary culture has always had an appetite for long, sprawling poems. We spoke earlier about sequences, but what about the long, through-composed poem? I remember some of your critics used to call on you for one. Has it ever been one of your own desires?

Well, sure, of course. What red-blooded American boy, et cetera. The disconnection of stanzas started in *Hard Freight* segued rather nicely into the sequences in *Bloodlines*. Then I wanted to do a book-length poem, a—as you just described it—"through-composed" poem. And I did, though one that was so camouflaged that almost no one noticed it as such. Helen Vendler did, and said so, and I'll always be grateful to her for that. The book was *China Trace,* and you and I talked about it somewhat just a little while ago, how each individual poem was a chapter in an ongoing story about a character who went from childhood to his demise and inscription in the heaven of the fixed stars. As I say, it was a series of short poems linked by an unspoken common narrative, a journey, even if it was more spiritual than actual. And that book, that poem, is where the idea of the subnarrative, the submerged narrative, started taking shape for me.

Now here's something that's kind of interesting, at least to me. Disconnection and association, as you so cleverly pointed out in your question, seem to be linked with the short poem—with the obvious exception of *The Cantos,* of course—and one thinks of Dr. Williams and Company. It was interesting to me to try it in longer reaches—not interminably, like *The Cantos*—and I've made several attempts at that since I saw it emerge in *China Trace.* The first time was in "Homage to Paul Cézanne," and it was fairly short and crude. Eight overlays, each different, hoping to form one consistent picture. In "The Southern

Cross" it got a bit more sophisticated, but it was in "A Journal of the Year of the Ox" that it became what I had hoped it might. The structural elements—the four entries about the Cherokees and the Long Island of the Holston, and the long sojourn in northern Italy—of "sacred places," as well as the natural one of the four seasons, plus the visits to the two great American medieval writers, Poe and Dickinson, and the two great Italian ones, Petrarch and Dante, et cetera, all combine to both hide and expose the story line, which is, like most story lines, circular. It deals with circumference, as Emily said her business was. It's mine, too, the outer boundary. In its way, "Ox" is a longer poem than the whole book *China Trace*, though probably not as vertical. Well, they are my two favorite things. Of my own, I mean. Which still, I guess, doesn't answer your question.

One of my problems has always been that I can't remember things that require sequence. I seem to remember only consequence. Which is to say I can't seem to remember ideas or principles or how to do things. I remember incidents, I remember details. Which is why, and here I'm trying to circle back to your original concern about long poems being done with the devices usually associated with short ones, all my long poems seem to me like short poems in disguise. But I suppose any nonsurface narrative poem will seem that way. Still, it's a way, isn't it, of keeping the pithy elements of the shorter lyric and holding onto the illusion of the long, effusive gesture. A kind of an American sprawl of a poem with a succession of succinct checks and balances. Epiphanic and oceanic at once. Intensive and extensive. The long and the short of it. Now *that's* American.

And let me ask you about getting older—that is to say, about the effect of writing experience on your work itself. I mean, you now know your way around a poem better than you did twenty years ago. Does that make it easier to write or not? And at the same time, do your higher standards make it more difficult now?

I suppose I'd have to answer "yes," and "yes." But it's not really that easy because I don't write the same kind of poems I did twenty years ago. So, in a way, I'm where I *was* twenty years ago, and the answer could be "no," and "no." Actually, it gets more difficult all the time. In the mid-1970s I began experimenting, in *China Trace*, with what I called, for lack of a better word, subnarrative—which, if I were Italian, would be *sottonarrativa*, "undernarrative," surely a more felicitous phrase. A story line, but one not always in evidence. But always a story line. In the poem "The Southern Cross" I started to get the hang of it, and I've been bending it and stretching it ever since. So it's *always* a poem, or a formal proposition, I don't quite know how to handle when I write it. Add to that the fact that one's ambitions, one's aspirations for the poem and what it can convey, are higher and harder to come to terms with the older one gets, so it's always a heavier load the farther down the road you get. I suppose if I were still writing the poems I wrote in *Hard Freight*, or the same *kind* of poems, the entire enterprise would be lighter and more acceptable, though not to me.

Since 1980, when I wrote "The Southern Cross," I have also actually *written* differently. Which is to say, I guess, *rewritten* differently. I've tended to do it more in situ, as it were. I get every section the way I think I want it instead of going back over a full draft of a poem. Perhaps it has something to do with the length, but also it has something to do with the concept of the poem and its ultimate reach. It's *always* difficult. Now and then. Beauty is difficult, Pound said, quoting Yeats. Beauty is difficult. So is articulation.

As for getting older, I don't see much to recommend it, except that it makes you despair more of ever saying what you think you want to say. So you work harder when you work. Otherwise, as I say, I see little to recommend it. Although despair is a kind of joy, isn't it?

I'm not quite sure I understand what you mean by "subnarrative." Could you explain it a bit more?

I'm not sure I can, actually. Undernarrative, *sottonarrativa*, is about as close as I can get. The smaller current in a larger river. The story line that runs just under the surface. It's broken, interrupted, circuitous, even invisible at times, but always there. Which is to say, it's not a "logic of image," or a balancing of blocks, or a "logic of the irrational," or whatever. It's a continuous story line by someone who can't tell a story. Subnarrative. Its logic is narrative but its effects are imagistic. It's like what Augustine says about Time, more or less: "I know what it is if I don't have to explain it. If I have to explain it, I don't know what it is." I don't know, it's just what I've come to do.

Can a reader be expected to know what is "in" or "behind" a poem? And if he can't, then can it really be said to be in the poem at all?

Well, I think so. I mean we're not talking about the Holy Ghost here, our Main Mover. We are talking about something that is, in a sense, tactile. It is there as surely as the story line is there in "The Pauper Witch of Grafton" and "The Witch of Coos." It's just not as continuously evident to the eye. I'll give you an example. When I was in China, we went by train from Xi'an to Chengdu, a sixteen-hour trip. One part of the ride was along the Jaling River, where the roadbed ran alongside the mountains. Many tunnels. Many, many tunnels. The landscape was particularly gorgeous because of the river and the crop patterns along it, as well as the flowering fruit trees. But we were in the tunnels so much of the time that the landscape became flashes of intense color and concentration as it emerged, hung there for a while, then disappeared as we entered another tunnel. And while it was in evidence, the color and patterns and design were twice as luminous as they would have been had they remained constant and usual. Each time the landscape appeared, it was unusual, but it was basically the same landscape all the way down the river, a constant thread that you sometimes saw and sometimes didn't, but was always there. I would hope that subnarrative, *sottonarrativa*, would work somewhat in this fashion. It is always "in" or "behind" the poem. What was the second part of that question? Weren't there two parts?

Yes. If the reader can't "see" the hidden narrative, can it really be said to be in the poem at all?

As I say, it *is* in there. If he can't follow it, or know it, I guess I feel he isn't concentrating. There are *always* signs, there are always the openings between tunnels. And even if there weren't, if the story line were submerged totally, like a mole, say, and all you could see was the broken path under the ground and no mole at all, would you really be able to say there was no mole there, or that there had never been a mole there? We're not talking about faith here, we're not talking about the Great Incarnator. We are talking about something visible, something you can see if you look for it. Even when it's least visible to the eye, it's there all right. In the poem—a place the reader must be as well.

You've just been using—I don't know how self-consciously—some religious metaphors, and they remind me of that strain in your poetry. Not just the metaphors and rhythms and diction, but the argument itself. The poems seem suffused with the stuff *of religion, but without any apparent belief—and it's the absence I mean when referring to your argument.*

They do, don't they? I mean seem suffused with the stuff. I guess because *I* was so suffused with the stuff, at such a high pitch, at such an impressionable age, and for such a long period of time—without ever believing it, really—it keeps coming back up on me. As though I had overindulged. The taste stays in my mouth, a taste that is not displeasing to me, but it is not exactly something I anticipate with pleasure. I think I probably would *like* to believe. I believe in belief, for instance. And it *is* the greatest myth going, isn't it? All those fabulous aspirations and assumptions! I mean, if it *were* true, what could be better? Everlasting life! I'll take a hit off that, thank you very much. Just because you don't believe it doesn't mean you don't like to talk about it, or think about it. Besides, I *do* believe in the efficacy of things unseen. It's just that I don't believe in this particular one. And there's no point in just believing in the trappings, in the manifestations. Flannery O'Connor was right about that, I think—if it's just a metaphor, the hell with it. Or words to that effect. I mean, what could be better than being raised incorruptible in the body like St. John?

Hmmm . . . Even though I don't have anything more to say, I feel as though I *should* say something else. I mean I'm sort of surprised myself it should seem so suffused with this stuff. After all these years of running away from it so hard, it's rather perplexing to find that it's invaded my subconscious like the invisible worm that flies in the night. Well, so be it. I guess if one considers, as I do, the true purpose of poetry to be a contemplation of the divine—however you find it, or don't find it—then it isn't so strange that my work is so suffused with the *stuff* of religion. We take the vocabulary we are given—in my case, Christian—and use it to our own ends. We try to develop and expand what we are given.

A contemplation of the divine. I guess that should include the textures of the world as well as an outline of the infinite.

I would hope so. Certainly that's what I've been saying for the last five years, explicitly, in the *Journals* I've been writing. And, for the twenty years previous, implicitly in just about everything I ever wrote. The textures of the world *are* an outline of the infinite. Stevens said, or at least I seem to remember that he said, the thing seen becomes the thing unseen. He also said that the reverse way was impossible. Roethke wrote that all finite things reveal infinitude. What we have, and all we will have, is here in the earthly paradise. How to wring music from it, how to squeeze the light out of it, is, as it has always been, the only true question. I'd say that to love the visible things in the visible world is to love their apokatastatic outline in the invisible next. I think all this, you understand, in my better moments. In my darker ones I'm afraid I rather think the way Philip Larkin did—not anxious for an "endless extinction." But we are defined by our better moments, aren't we? Surely we are. Otherwise, God help us.

And language, finally, is both texture and outline?

Language is the element of definition, the defining and descriptive incantation. It puts the coin between our teeth. It whistles the boat up. It shows us the city of light across the water. Without language there is no poetry, without poetry there's just talk. Talk is cheap and proves nothing. Poetry is dear and difficult to come by. But it poles us across the river and puts a music in our ears. It moves us to contemplation. And what we contemplate, what we sing our hymns to and offer our prayers to, is what will reincarnate us in the natural world, and what will be our one hope for salvation in the What's-To-Come.

Language, Landscape, and the Idea of God:

A Conversation (with David Young)

DY: I'm going to make the format of this interview open-ended. I will pepper Charles with a few acute questions and see what he comes up with. Then I'd like to segue into questions from the audience; having heard three papers on Charles and a reading by him, people no doubt have good questions of their own. So let me begin, Charles, by asking for some of your reactions to the three lectures on your poetry we heard.

CW: Well, they could have been a little more fulsome in their praise, I thought. [Laughter]

DY: I liked them too. Each one said very shrewd and quite different things about your work, and yet there was also some interesting overlap. One common emphasis that struck me was the idea that your poetry is quite religious. I wondered if someone who didn't know your poems very well might come away with a sense that it's obsessively spiritual or spiritualistic?

CW: Well, I don't know if there was too much emphasis or not. It is there, obviously. To be perfectly honest, I sometimes think it is more of an aura talked about than an actual point of ignition; which is to say, there is more smoke than fire. It's there, but it isn't as blanketing as it might have appeared to someone who didn't know the work, the poems, and who only heard the papers. But I think everything that was said was true as far as my concerns have been suggested. It's all there and I don't disagree with any of it. It's just that I don't think I'm quite as "dog-haunted" as Mike might have said. It's something that hangs over me but it's not a sword in my mouth. There *is* fire but it just doesn't encompass everything. There are other considerations. There are three things, basically, that I write about—language, landscape, and the idea of God. The idea of God seems to be the one thing that has floated up, naturally.

DY: Maybe there's no such thing as a really good lyric poem that doesn't have some kind of spiritual content?

CW: The idea of writing a poem, or writing poems, is a spiritual one and has been a spiritual one for millennia and continues to be one in good poems. Now what you do with that spiritual pull and where it takes you is going to depend upon the kind of poet you are and what your other concentrations or your nightmares are. Mine tend to be along the lines that were talked about, and other people may go in different directions, but it still means that every good poet is a spiritual poet to a certain extent. I suppose it's like (if you happen to have a spiritual tendency anyhow and you write poems) adding Valium to alcohol—it doubles the dosage. [Laughter] I double the dosage.

DY: Perhaps I had more in mind a sense that it could be misleading to overemphasize the extent to which Christianity could be called a dominant force in your work. I can imagine a paper that might instead have addressed your poems from the spiritual perspectives of Buddhism as the dominant set of insights or obsessions in your writing.

CW: I'm not a student of Buddhism, as you know. I've only read some books, but it is a condition of being that appeals to me, it is a search that appeals to me. Something, I might add, I am incapable of achieving. I know that. I cannot find that still, small center in my self or in the world that will make me at one with my world. But I look for it. In fact I look for that more than I would look for, how do I say it, a Christian resolution? I was brought up in a Christian atmosphere, of course, so my reference points, my linguistic touchpoints, all tend to be Christian. And so, since that's what I know, that's what I tend to adopt and use as best I can. But I would think, as I get older, my steps would be in the service of something more along the line of a Buddhistic journey than a Dantesque journey, as it were. You're right, that should certainly be factored in.

DY: Let me hypothesize yet another paper. This one would be tricky to articulate, but it would touch on the play and wit and humor in your work. The lectures did that to some extent, of course, but perhaps I'm saying that a good portrait of you has to bring even more firmly into the foreground the fact that you deal with spiritual issues and the appeasing of spiritual hungers, and at the same time you tease yourself, undercut yourself, parody and mock your own spirituality, so that one isn't sure whether one should take any of it seriously or not. I mention this especially because I think some book reviewers have overlooked it, not because I think it was absent from the characterizations of Stephen, Tom, and Mike.

CW: Well, I think they're all true. Self-importance may not be a cardinal sin, but it sure ain't a very good thing and it's something one should try to avoid. That is one of the problems of writing poems, maybe in writing anything, and maybe it's just one of the problems of living: self-importance, I mean. But certainly when you're writing, you have to put yourself in perspective and you have to put your journey in perspective. It's just a journey. I mean you're not there yet, you know; you never get there, and since I do tend to talk about things that are something you would not normally find in the newspaper, one has to take a certain kind of serious stance. But once you've taken that stance, you can't take it too far and so you start to undercut. You do this linguistically and you try to do it, as you say, wittily, from time to time. I think there's a lot of funny stuff in my work that no one's ever mentioned or maybe even ever seen. Of course, some people might say it's all hilarious; there is that too. But I'm not a preacher, you know; I'm not sure. I'm not convinced. I'm asking, I'm questioning. All of my assertions are questions. The poem that Mike read, for instance, had no verbs in it. What a ridiculous thing to do—to write a poem with no verbs! Even though it may be linguistically melodious, I think it's kind of funny not to have any verbs in a poem.

DY: That's a good example of your playfulness. The title of this broadside would be another one, would it not? How could people take totally seriously a poem called "Blaise Pascal Lip-Syncs the Void"?

CW: You don't take that seriously? [Laughter]

DY: Not the title.

CW: That's the most serious title I've ever written. [Laughter]

DY: It occurs to me that the titles are signaling a little more vigorously these days that people should be on the lookout for a mixed tone.

CW: Perhaps. That mixture of tone is something I've been scored for, actually, the fact that I tend to undercut myself at the wrong moments. Maybe that's true, but I'd rather undercut myself at the wrong moments than not undercut myself at all. There is a particular pleasure in thinking up titles, isn't there? There really is. I can imagine getting to the point where the titles are twice as good as the poem.

DY: Or you think of a title so good that you can't write a poem for it.

CW: I have a whole manuscript of those—poems I didn't write because the titles were so good. That title came about because of the famous hoax, that group that was lip-syncing its music, remember? Milli Vanilli was lip-syncing its music, and I happened to be reading, as I often do [laughs] in my old age, Blaise Pascal, and I got an idea, "Blaise Pascal Lip-Syncs the Void"—you know, that's hot, so I did it and wrote the poem.

DY: It's partly the way the diction slides around in that title. That helps prepare us for the tonal shifts.

CW: But you understand no matter what the titles are, the poems are still that same stuff. They're all about the same thing, no matter what the title is.

DY: That leads to my next question. I have before me these two books, *Country Music* and *The World of the Ten Thousand Things.*

CW: Hmm. Fabulous books. [Laughs]

DY: I think so: two terrific collections. I want to play around with comparing them a bit, and I can begin by asking you how you view them in terms of differences or similarities. Think of them sitting there companionably on somebody's bookshelf. Do they go together? Do they feel different? Do they represent a continuity?

CW: They feel like two sides of the same coin. They seem like a diptych of the same painting, which is to say, the same theme attacked from two different angles. They are the same journey ten years apart, basically. The same mountain, different paths. Technically, they are different and that's what, I think, made it possible for me to do it twice. I see them as two parts, I see them as a two-part invention—of a musical piece, as it were. I hope that there will be a third part. But I don't see them as very different things, no. As I've said before, the technical aspect of *Country Music* was in winding language down as tightly as I could and still make sense, and in *The World of the Ten Thousand Things* to let it go as lengthily as it could—the line, I'm talking about—until it ran up against prose but still didn't become prose. So I do see them as two fingers of the same hand.

DY: I'd like to delve into these two books. I love to test books by opening them at random. I'm going to do that with *Country Music* and *The World of the Ten Thousand Things* and ask you to read a few lines of whatever I open to and comment on what you find there in terms of technique and of content. This will give some specificity to our discussion of the two collections, and it will also introduce the giddy element of chance into these proceedings. So here goes, with *Country Music.* I have opened to pages 118 and 119, one of which has the poem "Wishes" and one of which has the poem "Quotidiana." Which one do you want to read and talk about?

CW: How about 120?

DY: Is that short too?

CW: They're all short; this is *China Trace*—there's no poem longer than twelve lines in the whole book. Shall I read the whole poem on page 118?

DY: Okay.

CW: It's called "Wishes."

> I wish I were unencumbered, in Venice or South Bay.
> I wish I were thrust down by enormous weights
> Anywhere, anywhere.
> I wish that the blood fly would crawl from its hiding place.
>
> The sun slides up through the heat, and has no dreams.
> The days drop, each nosed by the same dog.
> In some other language
> I walk by this same river, these same vowels in my throat.
>
> I wish I could say them now, returned
> Through the dry thread of the leaf, the acorn's root.
> It's somewhere I can't remember, but saw once.
> It's late in the afternoon there, the lights coming on.

Well, Mike Chitwood just talked about this poem in his paper, the idea of home as somewhere that you have been but you don't remember, or that you're going to but you still don't remember. It is part of a book called *China Trace*, which, I mentioned last night, is a book-length poem about a character who goes from one particular position to another particular position. This is one of the places, this is one of the stops along the way, and it's late in the afternoon there and the lights are coming on. These lights prefigure the lights in the last poem, in the heaven of the fixed stars. This actually was a fabulous choice because it makes clear that I *did* know what I was doing when I was composing the thing. It is a flow-through poem, a single poem, and all the way through there are points where the character, when he speaks, talks about certain things that lead to the end of this journey, and this is one of them. "Wishes." Obviously you wish to be there, to arrive, to complete the journey, to get where it is that you are going. Why that dog is there I don't know. But "the days drop, each nosed by the same dog" means the more things change the more they stay the same. "In some other language I walk by the same river"— that's pretty obvious, isn't it? Once you've got the context—you get there through the natural world, through the "dry thread of the leaf, the acorn's root." "I wish I were unencumbered"—I was writing that in the mid-1970s when my son was probably four or five years old and I was going crazy with the family business and wanted to be away. "I wish that the blood fly would crawl from its hiding place" is an impenetrable line. I have no idea what it means. [Laughs]

DY: So we can't ask you about that? You've signed off?

CW: I think I've signed off on the blood fly. Well, not really. The blood fly obviously is the thing that is going to lead you there; the blood is going to show you the way and the blood fly, if it comes out of its hiding place, is going to lead you on.

DY: Your account of this poem suggests that while it looks like a short poem, it's actually part of a long poem in a disguise.

CW: Right. I read from three or four of these last night, and I mentioned that each of these poems is a chapter in this pilgrim's book—that the journey this fellow starts in his child-hood eventually ends up in the heaven of the fixed stars, and he can't get any higher because he doesn't believe—that is, he only believes what he can see. Each of these poems is disparate but is a self-contained chapter; they are referential to each other and to the whole. Each one can be taken out individually, but put in place, in context, they make up this really weird long poem. It has a strange kind of flow-through quality to it.

DY: Now I've opened *The World of the Ten Thousand Things* at random, and I find myself on pages 98 and 99, one of which has "Homage to Cesare Pavese" and the other the first part of "Cryopexy," a three-page poem that's a personal favorite of mine. But we should probably discuss "Pavese" because it's shorter, unless you would really like to do "Cryopexy."

CW: I'll do them both. [Laughter] "Homage to Cesare Pavese." Cesare Pavese was an Italian poet and fiction writer who committed suicide in 1950 in Turin, Italy, on the surface because of a failed love affair with an American actress. She spurned him, and he said he never got over it and killed himself. But obviously, he had a darker side, things inside that led him on to do this. At one point in this book, which is called *The Other Side of the River,* I was working with other texts. I have a poem in here called "To Giacomo Leopardi in the Sky" where I talk about ten of Giacomo Leopardi's poems and translate and mistranslate parts of them and embed them in the text. I have "Homage to Cesare Pavese" where I take a very famous line of his and use that as the beginning of the poem. The line is *"Verrà la morte e avrà i tuoi occhi*—death will come and it will have your eyes." It's a very famous poem, at least it was in Italy in the 1950s when I was over there.

DY: Let me interject a question. Is the sense of "have" there that it will be wearing your eyes or that it will have them from you, take them away?

CW: No, it will be wearing your eyes. He's talking about this woman.

DY: The "you" is not the reader or the poet himself?

CW: No. "Death will come and it will have your eyes" and I assume it was always Constance Dowling, who was the woman he killed himself over. So that was the structural point of these poems: to try to use other texts within my own poems without taking them over completely, weaving them in, you know, in ways that Robin was talking about in the introduction. Do you want me to read anything of it?

DY: Yes.

CW: The first stanza goes,

> Death will come and it will have your eyes
> From morning to morning, sleepless,
> > an old remorse.
> Your eyes will be vain words, a silence
> You'll see as you lean out to the mirror
> Each day,
> > the one look that it has for everyone.

The last stanza goes,

> This is a balance sheet and the names don't count.
> One nail on top of another,
> > four nails make a cross.
> Nothing can add to the past—
> Woman is as woman does,
> > and night is always the night.
> With its black heart and its black hands it lays me down.

"Four nails make a cross"—that's the Pavese line from that stanza; the rest of it is mine. Now, "Cryopexy." A cryopexy is an operation on the eye to repair a tear in the retina; it's a freezing process. I had it done to me, to my eye, back in 1981. After they do it, they don't let you do anything for about ten days to two weeks except watch television. That's the only thing you can do because you never move your eyes when you watch television. You can't read, you can't walk around, you can't do anything, you can *just watch TV.* Or you can sit out on the front porch of your house if you live in California and look up at the sky and write a poem about light, which is what this is. The entire poem is about the effects of light coming into the eye. I was trying to write it like this [holds hands straight out in front of him] because I couldn't look down. I would try to visualize and make as concrete as possible what was going on with the blood spots as they moved across the surface of the eye and as the sunlight came in. And it goes on—God, it goes on for three pages. But I had ten days, you know. [Laughs]

DY: Read part of it, at least.

CW: Here are the first three and last two parts,

> Looming and phosphorescent against the dark,
> Words, always words.
> > What language does light speak?
> Vowels hang down from the pepper tree
> > in their green and their gold.

> The star charts and galactic blood trails behind the eye
> Where the lights are, and the links and chains are,
> > cut wall through ascending wall,
> Indigo corridors, the intolerable shine
> > transgressing heaven's borders . . .

> What are the colors of true splendor,
> > yellow and white,
> Carnation and ivory, petal and bone?
> Everything comes from fire.

> Sometimes, in the saffron undercurrents
> > trailing like Buddhist prayer robes
> Across the eye,
> > clear eels and anemones
> Bob and circle and sink back through the folds,
> Caught in the sleeve of the curl's turn.

Across the eye's Pacific, stars
         drop in the black water like pursed lips,
Islands and tiny boats
Dipping under the white lid of the strung horizon,
         this one in amethyst, this one in flame.

DY: Okay, now here's my little exercise, coming to fruition. Here is "Wishes," which we talked about, and here are "Pavese" and "Cryopexy." Right away, I see differences that interest me. The diction in the latter book, especially in "Cryopexy," is greater in range. There are more unusual words. There's more skidding around. There's a larger, more authoritative vocabulary that feels very much yours. You make it yours by bringing together words from wholly different sources and setting them in surprising conjunctions. No doubt there's a pleasing consistency in the poetic diction of "Wishes," but it doesn't have this unpredictable and soaring potential. Is that a fair assessment?

CW: Yes, it doesn't have the ambition either, I think. It doesn't have the linguistic ambition, trying to get more in, trying to say more, encompass more in the same amount of space on the page. Trying to expand your mind as you expand your line. But I think the ambition was the same in both of the books. I had more to bring to the ambitions in the second ten years. *Country Music* basically contains poems from 1970 to 1980; *The World of the Ten Thousand Things* includes poems from 1980 to 1990. So I hope I would have learned something or found a more recondite text I could steal from, at least have made some progress, you know. So that's a problem there. I also have to admit that even though I thought *Country Music* was ambitious, the poetic ambition in *The World of the Ten Thousand Things* is larger. The road that the journey was on was wider and longer, perhaps, than I had originally thought.

DY: I should add that I'm a great fan of *China Trace,* and that I'm not using it as an excuse to praise the later work in its place.

CW: Oh, it's still almost my favorite book.

DY: But isn't it striking to see how much your style has altered between these examples?

CW: I'm starting to get really interested in this line of thought because I had imagined the two books were almost the same thing. Obviously the language is going to be different because they're ten years apart, but there is more than just that; there is almost a difference in degree more than in kind. I would agree.

DY: What about rhythms?

CW: Well, once I got into this longer line the rhythms changed. These lines in *Country Music* look decently long, but they don't have that downstep line that changes everything and makes for a more ongoing sound pattern, a richer texture to the language.

DY: The language and rhythms of "Wishes" are somewhat formal and ritualistic because of the deliberate repetitions. But it seems to me that there is more fluency and fluidity in "Cryopexy." There's more sense that this could go anywhere, not only in its diction but also in terms of how it moves and behaves as a tracking of the mind, a mining of the imagination, a playing around with consciousness and its curious relation to language.

CW: Well, that's something I shouldn't respond to; I should just say "thank you." I would like to think that there is that sort of progression, that one has learned to tame it a little bit more, perhaps. I mean, we're all servants—but you know, there's the downstairs maid and the upstairs maid, and maybe I'm the upstairs maid by the time I get to here . . .

DY: Anything else about this comparative exercise that you'd like to comment on?

CW: I think both "Homage to Cesare Pavese" and "Cryopexy" are better poems than "Wishes" myself. It seems to be . . .

DY: If we had opened at, say, "Spider Crystal Ascension," instead . . .

CW: Something like that. This is more of a line cabin that you reach to show you you're on the right trail. Exactly. If I'd come to something like, well, "Spider Crystal Ascension" or "Reunion" or "April" . . . Still, the language is not as rich; it's a different kind, it's a different feel, it's a different weight to the diction, to the words, to the texture that shows in ways the poems go together. And I do think a lot of this has to do with the layering quality of structure that I started using in "The Southern Cross," which allowed me not to be so constrained in the way I earlier thought a poem had to be, so self-contained; therefore the language was more self-contained perhaps. As the formal apparatus opened up, somehow the textures and the linguistic abilities seemed to be able to loosen a little bit and allow more things in and allow me to run off at the mouth more if nothing else, you know.

DY: Do the covers of these two books tell the same story?

CW: They do, they do indeed. These are my two favorite painters in the world. *Country Music* has Giorgio Morandi's work and *The World of the Ten Thousand Things* has Paul Cézanne's. *Country Music* uses a very plain line drawing of a landscape, and *The World of the Ten Thousand Things* has a very lush oil of a landscape. Both done in the last years of the painters' lives and both done when they had gotten down to the essence of their art, without any kind of extras, just the essence. It also happens that the Morandi was done in 1959, the first year I went to Italy, which is another reason I chose it. It is more constrained than the Cézanne; the Cézanne is more open.

DY: Let me mention to the audience that Charles and I were talking about the Cézanne painting before the interview and I told him that every time I look at it it seems a little different to me. Sometimes the road is steep, sometimes not. Sometimes the image has great depth, sometimes it feels flat and all pushed into the foreground. I love that. I have pondered Charles' attachment to him. Like his attachment to Pound, it mystifies me a little.

CW: Well, more than that, it dumbfounds you. [Laughs]

DY: In any case, having this book around and having this cover to look at, I think I've begun to understand why you feel such an affinity with Cézanne, why you pay him such homage. And in fact, I like your way of paying homage. You've got lots of heroes, and you aren't afraid to say so. It's wonderful to let the people you admire, the writers and painters especially, people your books and get their homage. Still, let me just ask: why Cézanne rather than, say, Picasso, Braque, Monet, Matisse, some other great Modernist?

CW: Cézanne has a way of looking at a landscape that I find particularly innovative, revolutionary, and pleasing to my spirit. He breaks down and reassembles the landscape the way I like to think, when I'm working at my desk, I break down and reassemble what I'm looking at and put it back into a poem to recreate it, to reconstruct it. I like the idea that in fact he is very much of a realist although up close everything looks abstract. But once you get the right perspective, he is showing you just what's out there. I like to think I'm showing you just what's out there, but as I see it. I put these guys on my covers because I would like to get an inch closer to their genius, not because I put myself anywhere near their company. Also I like Morandi because he's very little known and Morandi's aim, his program, was different from everybody else's around him at the time. He sat there and he painted bottles and flowers and landscapes. When your subject matter in 1991 is language, landscape, and the idea of God, your aims are different from everybody else's. You're sitting there painting landscapes, flowers, and the edges of houses while everybody else is, you know, at the Super Bowl or whatever. So that's another reason

I like him, because he stuck with it, all his life; he stuck with it, and he ended up being the greatest damn Italian painter of the twentieth century, I think. He certainly was his own man and did it the way he saw it. So did Cézanne, not that you would want to spend much time around Cézanne, I mean, he was so obsessed.

DY: Somebody noted that the only poems you saved from your first book to include in *Country Music* were prose poems. He mentioned to me that you have said that the best poetry approaches the condition of prose, or something to that effect.

CW: No, I was quoting a phrase or a dictum by Eugenio Montale that I once read that I think is the truth about this. He said, "all poetry rises from prose and yearns to return to it," or words to that effect, and it is in that yearning to return to prose that real poetry is written. I think that's true. I do not think that poems are made out of prose. There is a certain stance that a poet uses when he writes, the diction is a little different, the language is a little different. It comes from prose and so you write in the direction of prose; you let it go back toward prose, and it is all in that tension between the two. Now that has nothing to do with prose poems. The reason I kept those five poems was that those poems seemed to me the only poems in my first book that had any kind of individuation about them whatsoever.

DY: So we cannot predict that the third of these volumes will turn out to be prose?

CW: No, I don't think so. No, no. I've put in too many years and run my mouth off too often in public about the sanctity of the line and what it means, and what it means to me, to get back into that practice. Steve and I were just talking about that yesterday, about what I am going to do. No, I am wedded to free verse. I am wedded to experimenting in structures and to lineal experiments—within reason. I don't want to get out into L-A-N-G-U-A-G-E P-O-E-T-R-Y. [Laughs] Did you say language poetry?

DY: And what about long poems versus short? Short poems disguising long ones, long ones housing short ones, paradoxes of form and length: care to venture a prediction?

CW: I think I'll probably go back to shorter things. I don't know how short—what I'm doing now is sixteen lines or less, but that's just one section. Then maybe I'll write, if I'm lucky, some one- or two-page poems, something like that. But no more forty-page poems, no more book-length poems. I've done that. I'd like to marry Emily and Walt again; I'd like to get the long line in the shorter poem, if I can. Whatever I can do that will keep me interested. I won't have another project like this two-headed project here, this double-edged sword, that I thought was the same and now I've just found I've been fooling myself about and it's not at all the same. [Laughs]

DY: I think I should let other people join in this process of asking questions, since Charles is being both eloquent and forthcoming.

Q: When you were talking about poetry turning into prose and back again, I was thinking of the quip that all great literature begins with gossip and goes back to gossip. Can we say that art begins with experience and goes back to experience?

CW: God, what a snake pit! As I said, I was quoting Eugenio Montale, and I'd have to ask him about this—but I can't yet. I do believe it's true, though it's the tension I was talking about, not necessarily that prose is lesser than poetry—just different from poetry—and that poetry comes out of it because of the essence and nature of language itself and it tries to get back to that particular quiescent state. But in its journey up and back, it is more charged, more filled with meaning, and that's where poetry resides. That's how I'm interpreting what he's saying. And if *he's* not saying that, then *I'm* saying that because I think it's probably true. More interesting than that to me is the idea of gossip—all literature starts with gossip. Take the *Divine Comedy*, for instance. When you read the *Inferno*, you think this is the most fabulous thing in the world, this is unbelievable stuff; then you read the *Purgatorio* and say this is better. By the time you get halfway through the *Paradiso,* you realize the *Inferno* has just been gossip. All these people he's been talking about, he's been making fun of and putting down; that's what's really going on. Now, I don't know that Montale had that sort of thing in mind. The *Paradiso* does not then return to gossip. So I would have to say if great literature begins in gossip, it ends in Paradise.

DY: We can mean so many different things by the word "prose." Is it that all poetry is written language that lifts out of the normal conditions of prosaic existence into something more expressive and concentrated? And that that is necessarily part of a cycle?

CW: No, I don't think it's a cycle. I think it stays up there and the yearning is the word. The yearning to return is where the tension and the energy and the excitement come into language, but it doesn't go back. No, it doesn't, and that would include prose poetry as well; a prose poem is a poem. It just happens to be written in prose, but it's a different kind of prose.

DY: Who's doing the yearning? The poet or the reader?

CW: No, the language is, and again I'd have to ask him, "Eugenio, my man, what do you mean?" The translation by Jon Galassi, from *The Second Life of Art,* is where I read this, and I liked it and I still think it's true. I can't really explain it, but I do believe that that is where the tension lies. I guess I believe that is where the tension lies because for the ten years of working on the books in *The World of the Ten Thousand Things* I was trying to take poetry and guide my poetic line in the direction of prose but keep it always from falling into prose. It goes in that direction, toward a conversational tone of voice, toward a prose kind of understanding of itself, but always stays just above, or just outside, and that tension, that keeping-it-apart is where the music in poetry lies, not in the completion. I like to think that the rhythms I'm using and the line I'm using keep it up enough from prose, and maybe that's why I'm so attracted to that particular statement by Montale.

DY: And the organizational mode of the journal is another central issue, isn't it?

CW: Yes. Absolutely. Keeping a journal, in which one is much more open, one is much more prosaic if you want to say that. But I do think that when we read journals, prose journals, we allow them more of themselves, somehow. It's just that the genre itself allows it. We allow them to be more candid, to be more self-referential, those sorts of things. That is good in a journal but maybe bad in a story or a poem. Therefore, if you take some of those qualities from a journal and put them in a poem, a book of poems, it always remains a poem and you can't cop out and say, well, it's a journal. No, there are all these qualities. But they do take on some of these other characteristics, and that's a huge risk because someone's gonna say, "Well, yeah, you know, talking to yourself, and all those other things, blah, blah, blah." Well, I hope not. One tries to avoid that, but one does know the risk.

Q: Would you comment on the significance for you of the term "halflife," which appears not only in your poetry but also as the title of your volume of essays and interviews?

CW: "Halflife" refers to prose. Prose has half the life of poetry, or my own does. Its half-life is also shorter. Or mine certainly is.

Q: Could you comment on whether or not you try to incorporate musical harmonics in your poetry or if you consciously try to exclude them?

CW: I don't try to exclude them, no. Unfortunately, I'm almost tone-deaf. I don't really know anything about music other than I like to listen to it. There is no way I could put particular kinds of musical harmonics into the line, but I try to use language itself in the arrangement of the words and the way the lines move to such an extent that there is a musical component to everything I write. It is very important to me. Ezra Pound once said about William Butler Yeats (Yeats was tone-deaf, too, supposedly), "He could get a tune in his head"—which indeed he could. He was able to exploit the innate music of words themselves, the sounds of the consonants and the vowels and the succession of them down across the pages. He put them together into a kind of musical movement. One tries to do that. I think one of the major conditions of good poetry is its musical component or element. But as far as being a musician, I can only talk about it; I don't know anything about it.

Q: This festival has had an Appalachian theme or flavor about it through the years, and I wondered if you could tie your poetry to an Appalachian theme or Southern theme or place yourself into that kind of context, or if you could give your response to the effort here to do that?

CW: I like that. It's the reason I'm here, because I grew up thirty-five miles down the road. I have always considered myself a Southern writer, and I consider myself someone who grew up in Appalachia, in Kingsport, right in the middle of it. That's important to me, it's really important to me, and so I am honored to be included in a list of Appalachian writers, although, of course, I don't want to be thought of as *merely* a Southern writer or *merely* an Appalachian writer. It has been really a fine occasion and I thank you, thank you all.

ET & WNC
Express Lines
(with Michael Chitwood)

[When Joseph Parisi, editor of *Poetry,* announced that Charles Wright had won the 1993 Ruth Lilly Poetry Prize, one of the most prestigious—and, with an accompanying $75,000 cash award, one of the richest—literary awards in the United States, he said: "Charles Wright has one of the most distinctive voices in American poetry. He is a master image-maker whose word pictures evoke haunting dimensions in the American landscape, particularly the South of his childhood." Wright, who has also won the National Book Award (1983) and PEN Translation Award (1979), is the author of over a dozen books of poetry, a collection of essays and interviews, and several books of translations.

Wright spent his formative years in rural western North Carolina and eastern Tennessee as his father, a civil engineer for the Tennessee Valley Authority, moved the family to different dam sites. Many of these little villages, constructed for the TVA crews and their families, have now vanished from maps, but they live on in Wright's poetry. In "Firstborn," written for his son, Wright tells the infant "The foothills of Tennessee, / The mountains of North Carolina, / Their rivers and villages / —Hiwassee and Cherokee, / The Cumberland, Pisgah and Nantahala, / Unaka and Unicoi— / Brindle and sing in your blood. . . ."

Wright spent parts of his youth in Sky Valley, Hiwassee Dam, and Murphy in North Carolina, and Pickwick Dam, Oak Ridge, and Kingsport in Tennessee. He was educated at

Sky Valley Academy and Christ School in Arden. He earned his BA at Davidson College (1957) and his MFA at the University of Iowa (1963). From 1966 to 1983, he taught at the University of California, Irvine. He did graduate work at the University of Rome (1963–64) and returned to Italy as a Fulbright lecturer in Venice (1968–69). Since 1983, he has been the Souder Family Professor of English at the University of Virginia. He and his wife, Holly McIntire Wright, live in Charlottesville, Virginia.

This interview was conducted in the third-floor writing room of the Wrights' Charlottesville home. The room is extremely orderly despite the large number of photographs and pieces of memorabilia the fifty-eight-year-old Wright has collected, including a recent photograph of the poets, including Wright, who completed a new translation of Dante's *Inferno,* and the doll's head Wright found in a field the morning he began writing "Homage to Paul Cézanne."

I began the interview by asking Wright about a recent poem, "Waiting for Tu Fu," which recalls a scene from his North Carolina childhood.]

Can you remember an organ chord one Sunday in North Carolina?

Well, I can remember a lot about that camp.

It was Sky Valley?

It was Sky Valley, between Hendersonville and Brevard. And I remember a lot of generic things. Various Sunday services on the porch of what was known as the Big House and in the little chapel by the lake, and so forth. The line you are quoting comes from that memory. It's almost from the same sort of remembered situation I mentioned years earlier in a poem called, I think, "Sky Valley Rider." The four grown-ups are sitting around the porch with their stern faces. This is the same type of thing. Mrs. Perry was playing the piano, so it wouldn't be an organ chord, it would be a piano.

"Organ" sounds better in the line.

Well, it also has two syllables, and piano doesn't. But, yeah, I remember that whole summer as one long organ chord. It has stayed there, and it reverberates every time I push it. It was a very interesting experience, to me anyway; I've been writing about it for thirty years.

That was when you were 15. Was that a pinnacle?

Well, yes, I was 15. I was there for about four years. That is, when I was 12, 13, 14, and 15. Four summers and one year. I started out as a camper at the boys' camp.

Was it a big camp?

Yes, oh yes. It was one of those big North Carolina mountain summer camps, you know. The Perrys had two of them. They ran a music camp for girls, on a main compound, and then a mile away was what they called a pioneer camp, a boys' camp around the lake with tents and cabins that they built each summer with the boys' help. That was part of the way they were able to make their physical plant, with the help of the campers, which was fine because it was good for the campers, too. I was there for three summers, I guess, until I was 15. When I was 16, I started working in construction with my father in Kingsport. But there was just one year I went to the camp and school together and then stayed for the next summer right before I turned 16.

The school part sounds sort of monastic. I mean, eight kids as you've said "under the evangelical thumb of the daughter of the Episcopal Bishop of South Carolina."

Well, that part was very monastic. There was one girl, who was a senior. She was studying music with Mrs. Perry. A girl named Ann Covin, whose brother, Bill Covin, I roomed with at Christ School the following two years. And then there was an older guy named Norman Richards who had graduated from Heath Springs High School in South Carolina and thought maybe he needed another year before he went to college.

Because it was such a small high school?

Because it was a rural high school. His father was the U.S. congressman from that district, so Norman had to go to Heath Springs. If you're a congressman, I suppose, you don't send your kid off to school. You want him to be there in your district. Norman was 18, and I was 15, and he was my roommate. And there were about three or four others. I guess there were five other boys, of various ages. Mr. and Mrs. Perry were the teachers. Mrs. Perry was a Renaissance sort of woman. There were two other people they had hired to teach who were conscientious objectors, as well as were the Perrys. The Perrys had gone up there as conscientious objectors during World War II and had stayed. This was 1950 or '51. So, yeah, it was rather monastic, for sure, but they always kept you busy. Since I had been there for three summers before, I knew the drill of the place, and what happened, what was expected of you.

Did you go there for that year because you had been going there for summer camps?

I think that's why I ended up there. I think I went there because my folks thought I was falling in with the wrong crowd in Kingsport, whatever that could possibly be in 1951. By the time I wanted to really find out why they sent me there, they were both dead so I couldn't ask them. So I don't really know why they sent me there.

But it wasn't a choice of yours?

No, it was not my choice—I was sent there. My mother was quite taken with Mrs. Perry and with the religious side of the school. I think my father was taken with the manly aspect of the place. I was sort of a hyperactive kid, as I look back. I know I must have been; I'm a hyperactive adult. So they probably thought it'd be good for me. I had loved being there in summer, at camps. I guess they thought I'd love being there at school. I don't remember hating it, but I did not want to go back the second year. They wanted me to but I didn't. I went to Christ School instead.

So the spiritual bent that is so much a part of your work now comes from your mother and, I guess, Mrs. Perry?

Oh yes.

At that point, it wasn't something you had thought about.

No, no. It was just sort of like osmosis, seeping through you. Of course there, when everybody was involved in this kind of business and Mrs. Perry spread that patina over everything that was done, it seemed very natural. She was a do-gooder, in the ways that were satisfying to her and were sometimes mysterious to younger people. But, a do-gooder in the sense that she really did care about world peace and cared about . . .

Sort of an early hippie.

Well, yeah, in an odd way, except that they were very un-hippie-like and very ascetic and didn't indulge in anything as far as I know except for OD-ing on the Episcopalian religion. Her father was the bishop of South Carolina, and her son was an Episcopal minister. They were just very much involved in that whole milieu; their whole lives revolved around it.

You weren't particularly interested in religion then, but it certainly came to be something you were interested in.

It came to be, I guess, because I got so filled up with it I was never able to empty myself of it. And as I said before, it did strike a certain chord in me. But I really did get my fill of the organized business there, and at Christ School. After that I never had much more to do with it. But it got into my DNA, I suppose. It must have; I passed it on to my son. He is much more involved in that than I ever was. But it was a good thing, certainly better than smoking crack cocaine.

I read somewhere, I think in Halflife *[Wright's book of essays and interviews], that you think of North Carolina and Tennessee as home. Is that because of the time at Sky Valley and Christ School?*

I'd say Christ School—Christ School and Sky Valley, and then I went to Davidson College; and there was also Hiwassee Dam, North Carolina, which is where my family lived when I was five, six, and seven.

Your dad was an engineer?

He worked for the TVA, was a civil engineer for the TVA, working on Fontana Dam at the time and living in Hiwassee Village. This was a little government town that had been set up overnight in the 1930s, in the middle of nowhere; I mean, Murphy was the closest thing to a town.

Which is not exactly what you would call a big town.

No! The closest village was a place called Farner, but apparently my parents loved being there, and, as kids, my brother and I loved it too because it was all this outdoor stuff. Those were always the happy memories that my mother and father talked about. . . .

Being in Hiwassee?

Yeah, oh they loved Hiwassee, and so naturally I loved it, and I have a lot of memories of that.

Pickwick, Tennessee, is the same kind of thing—it's just another little town?

I guess. I left Pickwick when I was six months old. There was nothing there at Pickwick when my parents came. The TVA built the dam and they built the village or whatever it was at the same time.

Have you ever been back?

Never have been back. I almost went a couple of years ago. I've been back to Hiwassee, about five or six years ago. I was reading in Cullowhee. The village is now called Bear Claw, and it's a vacation village sort of thing.

That's kind of what a lot of that has turned into.

Yeah. The lake was still there, and our house. They put different siding on it and painted it. It had white horizontal siding, and now it's green with vertical siding, but I knew it.

It wasn't hard to find the right place?

Very easy. I remember it very well. I was six and this is the first place that really imprinted on me.

You say in the Iron Mountain Review, *"My ultimate strength is my contemporary weakness—my subject (language, landscape, and the idea of God) is not of much interest now." Is Hiwassee where the interest in landscape comes from?*

Oh, I think that's where it all started, yeah. Because I was in the middle of a place that was all landscape. I was the "Last Non-Action Hero." I was put *into* the landscape, as it were. Akiro Kurosawa has a movie, I think it's called *Dreams,* in which a person who looks at a Van Gogh landscape suddenly finds himself in the landscape. I was put in a landscape, and I've been in one ever since. I don't know why that made such an impression on me but it did, and Sky Valley was a continuation of that some years later, and from there it was an easy step into the Italian landscape.

You think it was the remoteness of it, for a kid?

That's part of it. There was nothing there but the outdoors, a landscape. One building, a commissary downtown—downtown [laughs]—down at the bottom of the hill. There was a school, and then there was the community hall. And that was it.

Everything else was landscape.

Everything else was landscape and small houses up the hill. There was really nothing there. We'd go to Little Rock every summer, so I would get on the train in Murphy and go all the way to Arkansas. It wasn't that I was there locked in for almost two years, but the fact is that that's where we lived. I suppose some people would have hated it. If I had come from New York City and been dumped there, I probably would have gone straight out of my mind. But I didn't.

You spent your childhood in remote places?

We went to Oak Ridge, Tennessee, after Hiwassee, and that was a fairly booming little town during the war. We lived on a regular street in a regular house. Then from there we moved to Kingsport where we lived outside of the town. My father hated town. He always said there was no town he could imagine that he'd rather live inside of than outside of. After hearing that several times, you kind of take on that attitude yourself. I thought like that until I went to Verona, and Rome, and Venice. Now I'm not so sure [laughs].

Those are pretty nice towns.

Those are nice towns. But I don't know why landscape became so important to me. It may be that somewhere inside me, inside every poet, there's a painter trying to get out. I don't know. Inside every poet there's always something else trying to get out—in my case maybe it's a painter.

Some other artist, you're saying?

Some other artist, yeah. Or some other something. I guess inside of art students you know there's a philosopher trying to get out.

Or insurance salesman?

Well, no [laughs]. Maybe there's a teacher trying to get out. Inside of Eliot, there's Eliot wanting to stay there. In my case, it's been painting, and not just painting but landscape painting. I'm still fascinated by it.

And then there's the second member of the trio, language. Is that because that's what you had to express yourself with?

It's the only kind of music I'm any good at. Everybody wants to sing—everybody wants to play. And you've got to find something you can sing or play. The English language seems to be the only thing I can play.

Lee Smith said she wrote Devil's Dream *because she wanted to be a country music singer.*

She would come closer than I could, that's for sure!

I want to quote something now. "How sweet the past is, no matter how wrong or how sad. / How sweet is yesterday's noise."

Even when I wrote that I said, "Look, is this really true?" I mean what about World War II, what about Hitler, what about the Holocaust, they're not very sweet. I've always written about being young. And one's youth, one's past, is always, unless you had a terribly unfortunate time, something you look back on with a certain amount of pleasure, a certain amount of nostalgia. I equivocate somewhat on that statement because it isn't entirely true, but in my case it's certainly been more true than not, so I left it there.

Well, it sounded really Southern to me, particularly coming out of a book called The Southern Cross. *Was that book and that title an announcement?*

I suppose it was to a certain extent. I hesitated very much on whether I should call it *The Southern Cross,* knowing immediately that I would be crucified if someone didn't like it. But I was living in California at the time, and I was feeling very cut off from everything that I was writing about, and everything that has nurtured me, and everything that I felt was still nurturing me. So I decided to go ahead and do it. Obviously, I was talking about the constellation, the Southern Cross. Of course, I felt the Southern Cross; I wanted to be a Southern writer. I wanted to be thought of as a Southern writer even though I hadn't lived in the South since I'd started writing, so I said, I'm going to do it.

You felt at that point you hadn't been thought of as a Southern writer?

No, I didn't. I'm still not thought of really as a Southern writer. Fred Chappell, Dave Smith are Southern writers. It's odd because Dave has lived both out of the South and in the South for a long time, and Fred never left.

Dave's certainly back now, in a big way.

Yes, and deservedly so. I mean that they both are Southern writers in the good sense. But I'm still not thought of that way even though I feel myself to be a Southern writer, very much so.

I think you are. The Other Side of the River, the book of yours that got in my blood first, seems Southern in the best sense. However, it seems to me you are a Southern writer of a different kind. You haven't approached the topics and the language the way that Robert Morgan and Fred Chappell and Dave Smith and folks like that have. Did you avoid that consciously or was that a matter of temperament?

I guess it's a matter of temperament or a matter of ability as well. I'm not able to do what the people you mentioned can. Fred and Bob and Dave are all narrative poets. I can't do that. Narrative is the tradition; storytelling is the tradition. And I don't do that. At least on the surface I don't do it. And so, therefore, I didn't fit into a slot.

Which is the best way to be, not fitting into a slot.

I think it is. Yes, I think it is, but if you want to be a Southern writer that sort of excludes you temporarily until you've made the slot yourself. I was out of the South for such a long period of time, and, even though I was writing about it, I wasn't in the South where anyone would pay any attention to that fact. And since it didn't fit into the Robert Penn Warren, James Dickey tradition . . . there you go. I think Don Justice is of the tradition—how more Southern can you be than south Georgia? But he was in Iowa for all those years, and he was not considered a Southern writer until very recently. And still not in the same way that others are. It's odd that A. R. Ammons is; he's been at Cornell for all these years.

And Morgan's there too.

Bob's really never left Hendersonville, which is great. Bob's got a truly profound take on that area.

He doesn't repeat himself either, which is amazing.

Endless stories, you know, that's how he does it. He had a lot of relatives, and they had endless stories, and he hasn't forgotten any of them. Unlike some of the rest of us, who have forgotten everything. We spend our lives trying to remember, but Bob seems to have to forget some so he can concentrate on the ones he's working on. It's interesting to me that in an area that wasn't known for writers—the only writer who had ever been there, as far as I know, except for Wolfe, of course, was Carl Sandburg at Flat Rock—had, in my generation, at least a couple people there, right there in the middle of nowhere, which is a really fine somewhere. Bob even knew some of the people who used to work part-time for Mr. Perry up at Sky Valley, the Camp brothers.

You knew some of the same people?

Sure. It wasn't a big place.

And I guess any job would have been a good job.

151

Well, in those days, yeah. They worked part-time, and then they would farm hard scrabble plots. They would log and drive school buses and maybe work in mills. One brother, Hoyt Camp, was very strong. I remember he could carry huge logs. I wouldn't even be able to pick it up, and he could carry the same log twenty miles on his shoulders up and around the side of the mountain. They're just amazing. He was no bigger than me. He couldn't have weighed more than 140 pounds, amazing how he could do it.

I wanted to quote you something else. It's from your poem "California Dreaming." "Some nights, when the rock-and-roll band next door has quit playing, / And the last helicopter has thwonked back to the Marine base, / And the dark lets all its weight down / to within a half inch of the ground, / I sit outside in the gold lamé of the moon / as the town sleeps and the country sleeps / Like flung confetti around me, / And wonder just what in the hell I'm doing out here / So many thousands of miles away from what I know best . . ." Were you longing for Carolina and Tennessee then?

Oh yeah. I was looking out at the lights of Laguna Beach. I was just thinking that I don't really belong here.

The California landscape never did for you what the Carolina landscape did?

Never did a thing for me. Never a thing. I've lived here ten years now, and I've never written one word about the California landscape. I used to write about it when I was there, but just about the particular town, you know. Laguna Beach. It reminded me of Kingsport where we lived on the hill outside of town. The town was around Bays Mountain with the same sort of configuration, with the lights of the town around the dark mountain instead of the dark bay. The pepper tree outside the window reminded me of the mimosa tree in Kingsport. And so I was very nostalgic for back here, and of course like all nostalgia, it was like erotica. It was better reading about it, thinking about it, than it actually was when you got there.

So since I've been back, I've not written about anything in my past, my childhood, in the South.

Nothing about the South?

In ten years.

Because now you're here.

Because now I'm here, I guess. I've been writing about where I am, not the past.

Was it a conscious decision at the time, to get back to the South?

It was, but not just anywhere. I didn't want to go to the University of Tennessee. I didn't want to go to the University of Alabama or Georgia or any of those places. I probably would have gone to North Carolina; then the opportunity at Virginia came along. It was a conscious effort. My son was reaching high school age, and I didn't want him to grow up in a southern California resort community. Also, Irvine was the only job I had ever had, and I thought it was time to stir my stumps a little. See something different. It turned out to have been a very good move, because Holly found a permanent job here. Her career has taken off tremendously since she's been back on the East Coast. Luke [the Wrights' son] seems to have liked it, and I've got a better job. Actually, Irvine matched the job offer, matched the money and offered to give me a course off. What a fool. I should have taken it. If I'd known what a course off meant! But I thought it was time to leave. I have never regretted pulling out, even though Charlottesville turned out to be a boomtown. I thought I was going back to something like the size of Lexington, Virginia. Of course, I had remembered Charlottesville from, oh I don't know, the 1950s. It was much smaller then.

It was really about the time you got here that it took off.

It's amazing now. We saw in the paper yesterday, John Grisham, you know the writer from Mississippi, bought a big farm out here. There are more writers around here than you can shake a stick at.

Well, the same is true of North Carolina. Before we move away from the Southern business, I want to ask you about the tags "regional" and "local poets." They certainly have negative connotations. You can hear the "merely" in front of it. Yet, there are great poets, like Emily Dickinson, who barely left their room, much less their hometown. Is she a local poet?

I suppose I'm going to have to paraphrase Tip O'Neill here. All poetry is local. He said all politics is local. But all poetry is local. All writing is local. It depends what you do with it. She may have never left her room, but she never got her mind back down on earth. She is the least regional writer I can think of. I mean even Uncle Walt was more regional than she, and his regions were legion. But he was more regional than she.

She was so local she was universal?

She went out the other side, into that next universe, like a black hole, you know, just took all the matter with her. To get back to Southern writing, I came at it from a different angle than any of the other people you've mentioned because I think they came to it through literature, which I didn't. I never read English literature. So I became a Southern writer really by the fact that I'm Southern. I wasn't an English major in college, so I never read any Southern writers. I'm not saying that's a good thing, but I wasn't aware of the tradition, except for having read Faulkner in high school. I didn't know what that was all about, except that I liked it. That kept me from being regional in the sense that I really had no sense that I should be writing, at least literarily, about where I was. I just came to be doing it because that was where my heart tended to be when I was somewhere far away. I always wrote about it at a certain remove, not right in the middle of it. But I don't think I'm regional. In fact, I'd probably like to be more regional than I am. I think I'm local, but I don't think I'm regional, and I don't think there's anything wrong with being regional, as long as you don't overdo it.

Do you think that you can be taken seriously if you're regional, if you have the mules and the hoot owls in there?

Well, there ain't no more mules, you know, so I don't think you'd be taken very seriously if you write about mules and wagons now. You might have in the 1930s. The TVA came and electrified the Tennessee Valley. Things changed. But I don't know, there's actually quite a good young poet named Brooks Haxton, who's the son of Ellen Douglas. He writes very much in his first couple of books about Mississippi, about out in the country, but I wouldn't consider him regional at all. I don't really know why. Maybe it's because he doesn't live here, but he used to. I don't know what regional really means. I think it means that you have no reputation beyond two states, your region; therefore, it's pejorative. If you write the same type of stuff and have a national reputation, like John Barth, like Faulkner, it's a compliment.

Right, Flannery O'Connor is very regional.

She can leave her mule and wagon parked on the track any time she wants to. No one calls Fred [Chappell] a regional writer since he won the Bollingen Prize. So, I don't know what "regional" means when you have to ask somebody in New York or Chicago or San Francisco. So you're regional, and you've got a reputation one place and not another. I don't think it has much to do with you.

No. It's the way you're understood.

Harry Golden was a regional writer who owned the *Carolina Israelite*, a newspaper in Charlotte. He was a wonderful, interesting, amazing guy, who was regional on purpose. He brought his New York Jewishness down to Charlotte and just used to beat them over the head with it. He was funny as hell. He was wonderful, wonderful, and *wanted* to be regional because he was trying to bring something from outside into the region. So, he stirred up people. He loved Charlotte; that was part of it, too.

It seems harder for the emerging writers here to get the attention and awards they might get if they lived in New York or Chicago or somewhere like that.

The awards depend on who's judging. That's always a shot in the dark.

I wanted to follow up on what you were saying about writing since coming back to the South. You're writing more about intimate localities, your backyard for instance. Are you finding that the here and now is the surface of the hereafter?

I've come to understand that. The more you understand it, the more you think you understand it, the more you want to get involved with the here and the now, and that glittering surface, which has a pretty good shine all its own.

But it's in the particulars, isn't it—the minute particulars of the backyard that make the shine?

Yes, and it's not just the backyard. I don't think of myself as sitting on the back step, drinking a beer, marveling at the natural world back there, the tiny, tiny creatures [laughs]. That's not a very good answer for a very serious question, but then that's why I write the poems. That's the answer to a certain extent. You phrased the question so well that that was the answer.

I've heard you say that Hemingway was a person you read early.

I did read Hemingway.

And I see that so much in something like "A Journal of English Days" where you're walking through town. It reminded me of the first part of A Moveable Feast.

I've never thought of that, never made that connection between those two. But I love that first part, when he walks down the hill. Hemingway was very important as an antidote, as it were, to Faulkner. My tendency is to overdo, to put more butter on it all, you know, just lard it down with the language. Hemingway is just the opposite, and that's been nothing but good for me. I certainly don't pare down like Hemingway, and don't intend to or want to, but I admire what he was able to do with that. He couldn't write about women, but I sure like his dialogue.

The dialogue with the critic in Feast *where he's making fun of the critic: That's funny stuff.*

That's good. He is probably the prose writer most recognizable for his style.

You've said that after China Trace, *you started trying to get as far toward prose as you could, without becoming prose.*

Right.

Hemingway was a good model for that?

I suppose, except that I was using a longer, more conversational kind of prose than Hemingway would have, I think, approved of. But that would have been the model. *In Our Time*, that would have been the kind of thing I was working toward, the edge of prose. I was trying to keep it conversational but still to keep a sensible line, a steel rod through there, a reinforced line.

That's what I hear in Hemingway—a steel rod.

His is in sentences, of course. His sentences are almost—

—A line?

It's true. He worked on that for years and years and years, a way of building a sentence, in the same way that I, and thousands of other people who write poems, work to get a line together, for it to be a line and not just a bunch of words that happen to stop at a particular place. There has to be a reason for it being a certain way other than you just want it to be that way. That's not enough reason. Hemingway was a good model for serious writing. I don't give a damn about his lifestyle, but he cared about his writing in the early years. Well, he cared about it all the time. It's just that like all of us he started to repeat himself. You work your stuff over and over, and pretty soon you've worked it over so much it's working you over. You've got to be careful about that. You never know, I guess, after a while. I suppose if you get too famous, you never know. If you never get famous, you don't do it.

In your recent work, I've noticed an undercutting humor. Are you putting that in now to keep from parroting?

To prevent it, yes. You can take yourself too seriously rather than taking seriously what you're trying to do. And it's hard after you get older. You think, "Well, I can just say this." Well, you can't really. You can, but you better do it with the knowledge that you're probably not saying anything new, original, or even interesting. You hope it might be interesting, but you have to be careful, I think, that you take your writing seriously, not yourself.

You started letting more humor in with The Southern Cross, *which was your fifth book.*

China Trace, the fourth, was such a dead-serious book. It's still one of my two favorite books, I have to admit, but I felt I had to lighten up. That's when I started doing a longer line. I was thinking then, "I've got to watch myself, make sure I don't start preaching instead of praying."

There's the scene in "Gate City Breakdown" where the speaker has outrun the county deputies, and you say, "Jesus, it's so ridiculous . . . The way we remember ourselves. . . ." You give the serious or dramatic moment and then take it back.

We'd always love to see ourselves as the hero of our own movie. In fact, we're almost always the spectator.

Even in our own lives?

Even in our lives, the lives go on. I started to say the lives go on without us—what I mean is our life goes on without us to a certain extent. And, I think that, like the poem, the life has a mind of its own. You're along for the ride. Most people can't control their lives; they bounce right over the falls.

Lately, some of the titles you've been coming up with, like "Blaise Pascal Lip-Syncs the Void" and "Miles Davis and Elizabeth Bishop Fake the Break," are more broadly humorous.

Ever since I became an adherent of, or a member of, the movement known as Titleism—

Which you invented—

You don't have to tell anybody that [laughs]. My titles have been very important to me, and I guess I've gotten more invention out of my titles than I have out of my poems. Yeah, at least it's been fun writing, thinking up some of those titles. And some of them are not quite as funny as others, but for years I liked short, compact titles, one word, two words. Now I like longer titles.

Are you still going that way?

I'm trying to think of what's the last thing I've been working on, and I'm trying to think of what the title is—it was just the other day, and I've totally forgotten it. The one before was called "Still Life with Stick and Word." I sort of like the title, and this one is called—now what in the world is it called? Oh, it's called "Summer Storm," which I think is kind of funny because it's a meditation about a painting by Mondrian. When you're young, you think you don't need to title anything; it's all written so well, it doesn't need a title. Boy, titles sure help. All you have to do is teach writing for a little while, and you know how helpful titles are. You ask people, "Well, what is this about?" and the title has nothing to do with it. So, of course, now I'm doing exactly what I tell them not to do. The title has nothing to do with these poems. But I have a little currency in the bank, so I hope it actually does relate; at least I hope it does.

A contemporary of yours, Charles Simic, uses humor in his work as a balance. I've always thought the two of you had a lot in common.

Oh, he's a very funny writer. He's a very serious writer, too, but he's able to do it without falling over his feet. It's funny you should mention our similarities because I have thought that, too. He's very imagistic as a writer, as I am, and I find that I really have a lot in common with Charlie, really a lot. Our concerns are the same. We have the sense that it's all right there, trembling, right in front of you. For Charlie, it's usually behind a lit window at night or in a doorway. For me, it's under the hedge or up in the branches of the tree, but it's always right there, if you could just get to it.

This is out of an interview that I found in the Arts Journal. *It was 1988 and you said you were two-thirds finished with your work. Where are you now?*

I'm still two-thirds finished with my work.

And how do you know that?

What I meant was I'd just finished *The World of the Ten Thousand Things.* I had *Country Music,* which was the first project, and *The World of the Ten Thousand Things* was the second project, and I hope to have a third project. But as it turns out, I really don't have a third project, but I'm still writing. I would think that I will not have another project like those two, but I'll keep on writing poems.

Do you think there will be another book of collected poems like the first two?

Maybe. It won't be four books, I don't think. Maybe. Well, one, for sure, if I can get this one finished, and then maybe a second—who knows?

The one you're working on now, it's about finished?

It's about done. I'm writing now in sections as opposed to books or series of books. I'm just writing little sections of poems. I'm trying to finish this section called "Imaginary Endings." And I decided I wanted fifty poems in the book. So I've got five or six more to go. There are six sections in the book. The first one is called "Aftermath." It's twelve poems that are mostly a kind of overspill from *Zone Journals,* so they're like the journal poems with the same sort of subject matter. And, there's a section called "Terra Cognita," which means "known land," of course, and it's three poems about Italy in 1959. Then there's the section called "Broken English," which is four poems that are very discontinuous in form. They are broken even more than normal, than I normally do. Mostly, I open up a poem and stick something in the middle of it.

Is that like the sprung narratives you've been working on?

Yes, except "Sprung Narratives," the poem, is actually in the "Terra Cognita" section. It's about Italy, Kingsport, and Laguna. There's a section called "Rosa Mistica" where I tried not to use the first person. I think I used the first person one time, in all twenty poems. And then there are two poems about China. The last section is "Imaginary Endings." It's got four poems, so I guess I need five more. I kind of know that by the time I get to the ninth poem I'm going to have said all I have to say about imaginary endings.

Are you thinking of another group of books the way you did with books in Country Music *and* The World of the Ten Thousand Things?

The ultimate end of the first trilogy, *Hard Freight, Bloodlines,* and *China Trace,* seems to be a matter of subject matter to me.

The project in *The World of the Ten Thousand Things* seemed more technical, pushing toward that conversational language we talked about earlier. I don't know that there's a third side to be covered. I hope the poems I'm doing now, and the ones I'll do later, will somehow fuse those two approaches. It gets harder and harder, especially after fifty-five. I hope to keep on writing and not get pushed into prose.

I'd like to end by reading you something else. I guess I just like to read your stuff out loud. This is from "Lonesome Pine Special."

> The road in is always longer than the road out,
> Even if it's the same road.
> I think I'd like to find one
>   impassable by machine,
> A logging road from the early part of the century,
> Overgrown and barely detectable.
> I'd like it to be in North Carolina,
>   in Henderson County
> Between Mount Pinnacle and Mount Anne,
> An old spur off the main track
> The wagons and trucks hauled out on.
> Blackberry brambles, and wild raspberry and poison ivy
> Everywhere; grown trees between the faint ruts;
> Deadfall and windfall and velvety sassafras fans
> On both sides . . .
>   It dips downhill and I follow it.
> It dips down and it disappears and I follow it.

That road is above Lake Llewellyn, near Sky Valley. It was an old road even back in the 1940s. That was the road I was thinking about. You know North Carolina is in my blood. There used to be a trucking company called ET & WNC, which ran between eastern Tennessee and western North Carolina. You'd see the trucks all the time in Kingsport. They ought to put that on my tombstone: ET & WNC. That's where I came into consciousness.

Interview

(with Matthew Cooperman)

How has Laguna Beach been altered in your imagination after those catastrophic fires? You said about Oakland after the fires, quoting Gertrude Stein, "There's no there there." Does Laguna Beach feel that way?

Nothing is ever altered in the imagination or in the memory of that imagination. Once it's grooved in, it's grooved in forever. You may be different each time you revisit it—and, indeed, probably are—but it isn't. Laguna is as unchanged as Kingsport or Verona or Hiwassee Dam. As a matter of fact, it's probably more clarified and bulks larger by being restructured and partly disappeared. What isn't visible is usually larger in the imagination than what you can put your hands on, naturally. And if there is no there there, it is more here here—the more violently it vanishes, the deeper it devolves into its real place, back-lit and etched in the memory. Imagination is the great retriever, after all, memory's dog.

You taught at Irvine for seventeen years and returned to the South only in 1983. Is the notion of exile—imaginative exile—a force behind some of the longing for identity and place? And is your return to a more familiar terrain responsible in part for the greater foregrounding of literal place and people in your later work?

All poetry is written from an exiled point of view. Otherwise, why waste the time if you've never left or already arrived? And since most of us are only traveling through, it seems necessary that the imagination have a tactile place it can not only cotton to but identify with and rent a room in. Thus when we write home, we know where we stand.

Actually, the return to the South—which I assume you're talking about—and in fact, to Virginia, *is* responsible for, as you say, a more literal foregrounding (to use the jargon) of place in my more recent stuff. I presume you're talking about the "Journals" here, because that's what I'm talking about. The mnemonic glow was gone. I thought it was time to try a bit of actuality, and so I got the idea of the journal form, something quite immediate and aortal, more open to the tactile emotions (if that's possible) and the tactile landscape. What was, so to speak, under my feet and on my mind. That went on for five years, from 1983 to 1988. Once I got back here after the twenty-seven years away, I have never once written about the landscape of my youth—never once. It has always been of the present moment. I don't know what that means, but someone must.

And the foregrounding of people?

That came about because of a review I got once, the only time, I think, that a review has been generative. Helen Vendler said there were no people in my poems, and I rather liked it that way. But there it was in print, *no people,* so I decided to put some in. I did it mostly in *The Other Side of the River,* as people seem to go best with overt narrative, and I was trying a bit of that too. Then I felt I had done it, for better or worse, and went back to where I had been before. I'm not really a people person. I'm more of a landscape person. People are mostly, for me, merely foreground for what's really going on, always behind them.

In a recent interview (Paris Review, *#113, Winter 1989) you said, in talking about the twin influences, Pound and Italy, on your work, something like, "if form imposes and structure allows, then Pound imposed and Italy allowed." Could you talk about those influences as they have played out in your career?*

Reading Pound without interference was both a good and a risky thing. Since I had no instruction or history about either him, his work, or poetry in general, I really understood very little of what he was talking about. Again, both a good and a risky thing. The main thing I did learn from reading the Cantos and earlier poems, without having to be told, was that there was an obvious formal component to all this and that I had better pay attention to it. When I later found his prose writings, he instructed in no uncertain terms that this business of poetry is a craft that takes long in the learning, and that there are no shortcuts to the Muses. Form, the "making," orders and controls. The road forks and there are only two choices, form and chaos. The one is long and uphill, the other is short and an easy slide. Form is the imposition that sets you free. Pound imposed these ideas in the unmarked, fresh mud of my beginnings and they have hardened over the years.

The "idea" of Italy, meanwhile, allowed me free access to my imagination. The idea of a culture where art and writing and music were everyday things and occurrences—or so I thought—somehow not only permitted me to try my hand, but also sort of forced that hand as well. I have always felt that starting out in Italy allowed me to think globally while acting locally. It allowed me a freedom for the extended gesture if I wanted it. And eventually I did want it. Pound and Italy were a kind of concurrence of planets, as it were, that lit up my sky and showed me How and What. One is appreciative, to say the least, for such an horizon event.

I'm interested in your relationship to what Hyatt Waggoner has called the American Visionary line of Crane and Roethke. Is there a connection there and how has it evolved in your work?

Roethke doesn't really interest me much until his last book, *The Far Field*. And what interests me there is, of course, "North American Sequence," still an unacknowledged American masterpiece. I am, or was when I first read them some thirty years ago, much taken by their long lines, the sumptuous rhythms and undulations, and their subject matter. I can't imagine that these things haven't found their way, in some manner, into my own work. I like how he talks about the invisible world as well as the visible one. I admire his previous work, his more traditionally formal poems, but I am moved and persuaded by these last identifications with the animate and inanimate denizens of the landscape. What he thinks is important is what I think is important. I feel a kinship with these six poems, unlike any other contemporary poems I know. They are, you might say, singing my song, and I hear it.

Crane is another matter, more of an admiration, an iconographic desire. *The Bridge* is the Big Enchilada that you've got to try and reconstruct in your own manner. It is the American Gesture. The poem has some of the most beautiful language and music in our poetry. *White Buildings* is incandescent in many of its windows. Crane's "logic of metaphor" is not always logical, of course, which is its seduction. Directness of meaning, accessibility, has never been the major aim of poetry and/ or poetic form. Other felicities very often predominate in the first pressing. Meaning can come more strongly in the second or third. Wine is fine, to continue the image, but grappa's the whapper. Crane is the mountain, Roethke the valley; each comes out of the other in my landscape.

You quote Auden in Halflife *as saying "Truth is Catholic, but the search for it is Protestant." How is that so, and how is that alive in your poetry?*

Well, I suppose you could say that the Catholic Church is the descendent and heir of the original church, the only and first church, therefore if there is a truth to be found, such a truth would reside there, and not in its tributaries. Being Protestant, one would always stand in the tributarial position and, if one were trying to get back to the original source, the truth, one would always be attempting to go back upstream, against the current, mapping the length of the tributary to its source. So the search is Protestant, since the source just *is*. But that's not how he means it, surely. Surely he meant something more metaphoric, being the good Anglican that he was, a major tributary if there ever was one. And being good Anglicans, metaphorically, we all have to work hard to find the truth, I suppose, which is there for the knowing if you pursue it diligently enough in the right place. The search is, I hope, alive in my work the same way it is alive in my life—the bell that calls me from over the mountain. And unlike Mallory's mountain, some of us climb this one because it's not there.

Could you discuss your search for the sacred relative to your upbringing? Was that failure of a traditional belief system the beginning of another and does it hinge on doubt? How has that shaped you?

I don't really know, even yet, how that has played out. I don't know whether, since I was cut off from one belief system (self-cut, I might add), it led me to pursue my own version so avidly in my writing, as though I were trying to explain and justify my early action to the people who were so intent on my remaining faithful to the original (i.e., the church)—my mother, Mrs. Perry at Sky Valley, Father Webster at Christ School—, or whether it's just in my nature to do what I do. I suspect it's some combination of the two. Also, I've forgotten my upbringing almost entirely by now, and it might be that I'm merely seeking refuge in my writing from the vicissitudes of human relationships the way others seek equal refuge in the church. Of course, I don't think so, but you never know—the get-thee-to-a-nunnery syndrome. In my case, a verbal monastery. Whatever, the search for the sacred does continue. It is the unicorn with the golden horn, and makes most other searches seem lightweight and worthless.

You mentioned doubt. Everything hinges on doubt. Without a beginning in doubt, there is no faith. Thomas is the main man here. Without Original Doubt there is no future acceptance. As far as another belief system, it's the same system, just a different code. And as any old intelligence agent will tell you, nothing matters but the codes. Cryptography is all. You get the right code, you discover the secret.

And how has doubt shaped me? The way the Pacific wind shapes the Pacific cypress, the Monterey cypress—to its own will and its own desires. Both of which, of course, are blind.

The idea of journey, both in and out of the body, in and out of the autobiographical self, is a persistent theme in your work. I'm thinking of all the work, really, but particularly Bloodlines *and* China Trace, *the "Pilgrim's walking to and fro." This journey, and the "pilgrim's progress" if you will, seems a primary concern, and one integrally woven up with the sacramental urgency in the work. What is the importance of this "journey" and how does it operate in your poems?*

The importance of it is just what you have said in the question, and in the last question too, if I remember it rightly. It has to do with where the journey goes, and how it works. It goes in and out of the body, it goes in and out of the autobiographical self (or, at least, the putative autobiographical self). It involves a transubstantiation of things, people, and places as well as of a metric. Which is to say that the formal conditions are transubstantiations of the content, the content being what it all means, somehow. The formal elements are a reconfiguration of the moral values inherent in meaning. The ultimate importance of the journey is the same as it was in the search in the previous question. The journey itself, naturally has interests and adventures—adventures in language, adventures in subject matter, adventures in meaning—all along the way. But the end of the journey is what is important. The tracks of the unicorn are exciting, a glimpse of the glitter of the horn is exciting, but they are both second best. Best is the breath of the unicorn on your own face. The journey is, in one way, the path along the river of blood, as Dante had it in the *Inferno*. It's also up the river of light, as he also had it in the *Paradiso*, where one hopes to wade one day, upriver, undeterred. As far as my poems go, it is the road, it is the undernarrative, the *sottonarrativa*, that runs under the entire overlay of my work, the one unvarying direction that holds the parts and stations together. It takes me where I have to go.

The sense of the long poem is curiously immanent in your work. By curious I mean the level of accretion, from poem to poem, book to book, collected volume to collected volume, as if "the journey of the poet" was irreconcilable to an ending. And yet you manage to do that in books that change radically in form and structure, and almost entirely within a lyric framework. As sustained work, that seems unusual. Could you discuss that?

Well, not irreconcilable to any ending. "An" ending, perhaps. But "the" ending, certainly not. As I've been saying, "the" ending is where it is headed for. That end, as in any pilgrimage, is, of course, death, and I do expect to arrive. What I'll have to say on the subject remains to be seen. Or heard, as the case may be. Then, someone else would have to know the code, and that's, as they say, unlikely. Globed Fruit City, no doubt.

Writing two extended, interlocking, interdependent works has been my obsession and task for about twenty years, from the early 1970s to the late 1980s. And since a lyric framework was all I knew, and all I was capable of, given my inclination toward, and dependence upon, submerged narrative, I was forced to work within those constrictions. Or to make such constrictions elastic enough to keep me between the ditches and at the same time extend the road indefinitely. The challenge was to sustain disparate books individually and collectively at the same time. The structure of *Country Music*, the trilogy headed upward, was one way. The other, in *The World of the Ten Thousand Things*, came into play when the idea of the Journals took over. That idea was retroactive structurally, as it happened, and pulled the first two books, *The Southern Cross* and *The Other Side of the River*, along with it and gave them, in retrospect, "journal" status as well, even though their movements are generally otherwise. I find the journal format, at least as I've tried to use it, and reinvent it, that strong. Perhaps it has something to do with the shared lineation movement in the first two books and the second two. Perhaps it's the discontinuous structure of the individual poems, held together by that *strada sottonarrativa*, the undernarrative road they are all traveling over, both literally and figuratively. The journey holds us together. The destination sustains us. I hope, in any case, that the designation "extended work" is accurate. I have worked on the books with that in mind. The projects evolved on two levels, actually. One was subject matter, which we've been talking about for some time now in the other questions, and the form the subject matter took. The other level was more visible and audible. I tried to make the poems as condensed and compact as possible in *Country Music,* from prose at the beginning to an almost elliptical condensation in *China Trace.* Then, having squeezed the visible form into a ball, as it were, I tried to unwind it and stretch it back out in the direction of prose, conversational, at the end taking a prose convention, the journal, as a framework, but working within it in poetry, a poetic line, to keep it shy of prose. The substructure, the subject matter, continued to be what it had been in *Country Music,* but with different clothes on. The content was unchanged. It was still the same road. In *Country Music* it went up the mountain. In *10,000 Things* it goes down the valley.

I am fascinated by your sense of "communion with the dead," particularly in The Southern Cross *and* The Other Side of the River. *These personages strike me as both specific and generalized, personal memories and a numinous beyond, a way of seeing, but also a way of remembering. Would you say that is accurate?*

I would say this is accurate, yes. When I talk to Giacomo Leopardi, for example, it's more of a way of paying tribute to him as a writer, and what his writings have meant to me. Not too much feedback, either, as you might expect. I suppose there is some sense of retrieval going on in other cases, dredging the waters of memory, as it were, for those I once actually knew, as opposed to someone whom I only admired but never knew. But poetry has always been, on one level, a communion with the dead, hasn't it? One often writes to impress them, to sing to them, to let them know you're around, if nothing else. Besides, as I said once before, they've got all the answers, don't they? Poetry so often rises out of previous poetry, rather like new vegetation out of old vegetation, enriched and informed by what's dead. So in that way, we're always in a constant communion, eucharistically, with the dead.

Could you discuss the evolution of your line through the years?

There hasn't been much of an "evolution," actually, it's just gotten longer. Its tensility has been stretched, rather than compacted, though I like to think it's just as strong, though in a different way and to a different purpose. The first time I ever had any "sense" of a line as a line was when I started writing syllabics about thirty years ago, in 1963. It was the first time I had ever felt comfortable in lineation, and was doing something I felt was compatible to the way I thought, or felt I thought. I am still using a line that is syllabically based. It's true I try to manipulate the stress patterns within this syllabic framework, but the overriding urge and discipline is syllable count, almost always in odd numbers, anywhere from three to, say, twenty-one in a line. I count every syllable, every time, in every line I write. I suppose it's an evolution of sorts to go from a patter, an even patter of syllabic lines to an uneven series of syllabic lines. If so, my line has evolved. If not, not. As I say, it's just gotten longer, a kind of half-free verse, I suppose.

As your poems have become more discursive they've also become more transparent in terms of the writer's "being seen." Particularly in Zone Journals, *the personal moves to the forefront. As the barrier between prose and poetry begins to dissolve, the distinction between the highly crafted poem and the private journal dissolves too. Perhaps it was an inevitability once you began "unraveling the spiders' web" from* China Trace. *What has been behind that evolution?*

The form itself, I suppose, more than anything else. The taking of a prose "attitude" (the idea of a journal that was not merely diaristic) to perform a poetic function. The taking of a prose genre to promote and enhance a poetic occasion. The taking on of a prose way of speaking to engender and personify a poetic "voice." The taking on of a prose structure in order to restructure the poem. I'm not really sure that barriers dissolve, but repositionings become possible, openings become possible. One feels, in a way, more available to one's emotions, somehow, with this traditionally "tell-it-like-it-is" structure which the journal affords. At the same time, one— at least I do—feels even more obligated than ever to keep the

171

poetic virtues strongly in hand, so that one is working as tightly as possible in a more open venue. In my case, my longtime ambition to be Emily Dickinson on Walt Whitman's open road, kinetic compression within a more open-ended space. The poetic charge remains the same, but the emotional quotient is altered a bit and placed in the foreground a bit more. Even though the journal poems are different in conception and even in structure, they can't be different in execution or in formal values. They are always poems and arrive always with that attendant obligation. They just have a lot more on their mind, and feel freer to speak that mind.

If the journals allow for a more conversational, open format, the way they are composed would seem to require a different technique also. For instance, composition by line versus composition by stanza.

Composition by line has always been my game. Always. Except when I wrote the few prose poems I've done, and then it was sentence by sentence. There are writers who compose their lined poems sentence by sentence. Such poems have a prosey ring to my ear. Hopkins scanned from stanza to stanza, though I suspect he composed linearly. Williams said the stanza, not the line, was his unit of measure. But that was part, as I recall, of the variable foot project, so I can't be quite convinced. I suppose if you are writing surface narrative, it's easier to compose by sentences and, to extend that, by paragraphs. At least I would imagine the temptation to do so would be great. Since my sense of narrative is subterranean, the line works best for me, a series of building blocks, or strokes, or layers that tend to accrue rather than be directed.

How do you compose nowadays? Is there a routine, both to the original inspiration, what it produces, and to the final form, revision?

I seem to revise as I go, line by line, getting the line right before I go on to the next one. I never, it seems, finish a poem and then go back and revise. Composition and revision go on simultaneously. Odd. Lineation. I build them line by line until they are freestanding.

Your work has often been called "painterly" and, indeed, your avowed love of Cézanne and Morandi, among others, supports that. I like your comment on Matisse, too, it's not "how you put it together, but how you keep it apart." Could you talk about that?

There is a kind of spatial negation, a visual power in absence that painters understand and employ, and which I'm interested in poetically. It's a sort of white hole that has a kinetic draw to it that the lines of the poem float on and resist. Part of my interest in the dropped line for me is that it sets up a bit of this power field within the line itself; a rhythmic jolt sometimes might appear, small as it is, that kicks the line and the poem along, keeping it alive over the top of a force that would founder and sink it at any time. But everybody knows this. You keep the composition apart just a little to let this energy in and out, and to let the poem in and out of the energy generated by this emptiness. It's all about the same thing, the power and domination of what's not there, the energy of absence.